★ ★ ★ ★ ★ ★

PCS TO CORPORATE AMERICA was written specifically for the military officer and is the most powerful tool on the market today for any officer considering a permanent change of station to Corporate America.

PCS TO CORPORATE AMERICA was written by Roger Cameron, the leader in the placement of military officers in the private sector. Roger has successfully located civilian careers for military officers throughout Corporate America for over 27 years.

PCS TO CORPORATE AMERICA and Roger have been recognized worldwide as the authority on career transitions. Spotlighted on CNN and all major network affiliates, Roger has also received acclaim in publications including *FORTUNE, The Wall Street Journal,* and *The Stars and Stripes.*

PCS TO CORPORATE AMERICA combines years of research in one handbook. There is no other source of information available on the market today which provides the wealth of information contained in just this one book.

PCS TO CORPORATE AMERICA explains what to expect during the entire career search process — including resume writing, interviewing preparation and techniques, and the follow-up process, through job offer and acceptance.

PCS TO CORPORATE AMERICA will give any officer the competitive edge to get the job he or she wants in today's marketplace.

★ ★ ★ ★

"Read this book! Roger Cameron is an expert on preparing military officers for successful careers in Corporate America. Regardless of whether you're interested in engineering, marketing and sales, or manufacturing, listen to him. He'll guide you through the entire process — resume, application, interviews, and job offer acceptance. Bottom line: Roger Cameron knows exactly how to help you make it happen in Corporate America."

> — Mark Beyer
> Manufacturing Manager
> General Mills, Inc.

"Roger Cameron and Company are a first class act. **PCS** is excellent, his talks are inspirational, and his friendship is genuine. He can teach you not only how to transition from the military to a successful corporate career, but also how to interact effectively with people throughout life. If he ever retires, he should teach leadership at The Naval Academy. Don't leave the military without reading **PCS** first!"

> — Charles Kineke
> Senior Consultant
> KPMG Peat Marwick

"Roger and his team embody professionalism. Because of this professional preparation, I was prepared to successfully convince the recruiter that I could take on a very technical role with a 5-year-old degree. Procter & Gamble is a highly professional company and I was prepared for the difficult questions focusing on my ability to integrate into, and impact on, the company. Roger does not 'sugar coat' a thing — he knows how to 'make it happen.' Listen to his advice. Read **PCS**. It certainly paid off for me."

> — Lorraine Withers
> Process Engineer
> Procter & Gamble

"You must not only learn what Roger teaches you within these pages, you must internalize it!!! The skills and tools Roger introduces in his book must become part of your individual skill package — for this will not be your final interview, rather the first of many in your career."

> — Michael Lover
> Area Manager
> Pizza Hut, Division of PepsiCo

"**PCS** will provide you with your plan of action. The earlier you take its insights and advice to heart, the better off you will be. You will read this book over and over as you work, and I mean work, toward your transition. My husband, a former JMO and an MBA candidate at the #2 business school in the country, uses **PCS** as his interview preparation bible. There simply is no better guide!"

> — Kris Fuhr
> Associate Brand Manager
> Kraft General Foods

"*Roger's clear guidance in* **PCS** *greatly aided my ability to assess my capabilities and how they would transfer to the civilian world. Follow and use* **PCS** *as your handbook and you'll be well on your way to a successful career transition.*"
>   — *Bill Spear*
>   *Facilitator*
>   *Ethicon Endo-Surgery, Division of Johnson & Johnson*

"*To the point, substantive advice.* **PCS** *was my 'bible' during my transition from the military to Corporate America. For direct results, unequivocally one of the most reliable sources! I will continue to use* **PCS** *again and again throughout my career.*"
>   — *Patty Mills*
>   *Operations Resource Manager*
>   *Frito-Lay, Inc., Division of PepsiCo*

"*I have known Roger for over 13 years. Roger prepares his candidates to communicate their abilities and make the best use of my interviewing time.*"
>   — *Jim McGinnis*
>   *Client Representative*
>   *Corning, Inc.*

"*No one has a better understanding of what it takes to be successful in Corporate America. Roger's 27 years of experience in the military officer industry makes this a must-read book for the transitioning professional. As an ex-military officer, I wish* **PCS** *had been available when I began my corporate career.*"
>   — *Ed Clark*
>   *Manager, Commercial Sales*
>   *SimuFlite, Inc.*

"*As a recent JMO leaving the military for the corporate marketplace,* **PCS** *was my source of inspiration and guidance. Using* **PCS**, *I was able to gain a thorough understanding of myself and what has made me successful.* **PCS** *enhanced my ability to articulate my accomplishments clearly and concisely in the corporate interview. I prepared for Corporate America with this book and, very simply, I would not be here today without* **PCS** *and Roger Cameron.*"
>   — *Chuck Alvarez*
>   *Sales Representative*
>   *Becton-Dickinson*

"*Roger Cameron knows exactly how to help military officers excel in corporate interviews. He is painfully blunt and totally correct on every detail needed for successful transformation to a civilian career.*"
>   — *Judy Partin*
>   *Process Engineer II*
>   *Georgia Pacific*

"I transitioned to Corporate America through Roger because, quite simply, he is the best! He not only prepares you for the interview, but challenges you to grow as an individual during the preparation and interview process. After reading *PCS*, you will be a more positive, goal-oriented, energetic individual."
> — Tim Carlin
> National Sales Manager
> KFC, Division of PepsiCo

"Roger drills you on what works, what doesn't work, and gives you that much needed confidence boost. In PCS, Roger provides the knowledge, skill, and attitude in proper balance. Don't kid yourself, failure to prepare is obvious, and limits your possibilities. Master this book, listen to Roger, and make being prepared second nature."
> — Tom Anderson
> Sales Trainer / Representative
> Ethicon Endo-Surgery, Division of Johnson & Johnson

"*PCS to Corporate America* was of tremendous value to me during my career search. By studying and practicing the techniques contained in the book, I learned to communicate my past accomplishments and experiences with greater clarity and brevity. The added skills and self-confidence I acquired after using *PCS* resulted in my success during follow-up interviews. I strongly recommend this book to those officers leaving military service."
> — Timothy Goodly
> Employee Relations Advisor
> Mobil Exploration & Producing U.S., Inc.

"Roger, through *PCS*, helped me be comfortable and confident in 'me' and truly believe, 'Yes, I can!' Thanks, Roger."
> — Kristi Blanchard
> Data Processing Manager
> Wal-Mart Stores, Inc.

"Roger mesmerized us in Frankfurt, Germany, almost 13 years ago with his revelation of opportunities in Corporate America. Fast-track promotions, pay for performance, and recognition of ability have all come my way. Roger's skills are reflected by his recruits in their ability to quickly take on responsibility with overwhelming confidence. I am indebted and proud to be a successful alumnus of his program."
> — Ray Sears
> Senior Engineer III
> Halliburton Services

"When you apply what Roger and *PCS* advise, you will be in Corporate America. I am often asked who is the best in the business and I always tell them — Roger Cameron — there is no other."
> — Andrea Dillard
> Account Manager, National Marketing Center
> Burlington Northern Railroad Company

"*Roger exemplifies the passioned professional in his approach to sourcing and placing military officers. In 20 years of working with him as a JMO and later as a professional recruiter, I consider him to be the best at his craft.*"
— *George H. Jenkins*
Supervisor of Conference Services
Mobil Exploration & Producing Technical Center

"*Roger has been a pioneer in the business of transitioning military officers to the point of actually helping create the market. It's no wonder he is so dominant in attracting and positioning military officers for top industry. During the pressurized format of a corporate interview, Roger's sense of anticipation and preparedness gave me a definite edge.*"
— *Ralph Pavek*
Plant Manager
Quaker Oats

"*In my preparation for the job market, Roger made sure I had all the necessary information to make an informed decision. He helped me take a good hard look at myself and what I have done in my life to make me successful. Roger knows what it takes to be a success.*"
— *Troy Barring*
Operations Director
Fairchild Aerospace Fasteners

"*Roger Cameron is your most valuable source for accurate information about what skills the job market requires. His advice was instrumental in my getting the great job I have today. Use your time in the military to apply Roger's advice to build a strong foundation which will place you head and shoulders above other officers who have failed to prepare for entering the job market.*"
— *Laura King Elliott*
Materials Management
Ethicon Endo-Surgery, Division of Johnson & Johnson

"*No one can prepare you for your transition from the military to Corporate America better than Roger Cameron. I read several books in preparation for my transition; however, none compared to PCS. Roger's expertise not only prepared me to make a smooth transition, but has also helped me excel in Corporate America. Anyone planning to separate from the military must read this book.*"
— *Roger Martinez*
Warehouse Shift Manager
H. E. Butt Grocery

"*PCS is the best interviewing handbook on the market today, and should be the first book you read before beginning the interview process. It will focus your efforts to maximize the use of your time. Nothing in the book should be overlooked. PCS is your road map for the most complete preparation available to the interviewee.*"
— *Scott Milliren*
Project Engineer
Helmerich & Payne International Drilling Company

"In **PCS**, Roger provides a superb instructive counsel and an inspirational message for all JMOs contemplating a career in Corporate America. He provides a unique combination of valuable, practical information for interview success and a wonderful philosophy for living each day with enthusiasm, optimism and honor. Follow Roger's advice and you will be wildly successful!"

    — *John Grisillo*
       Regional Maintenance Manager
       Schneider National, Inc.

"Roger Cameron's book, **PCS To Corporate America**, is an engrossing and powerful read, but the book is most effective when it is used as a tool. I read **PCS** before I decided to leave the military. I studied and worked the exercises while I was preparing for my transition, and I referred to it countless times during the interview process. **PCS** helped me to land the job that I really wanted!"

    — *Debra Egloff*
       Process Support Engineer
       Applied Materials, Inc.

"I have known Roger from both sides of the interviewing couch. As a former military officer who became a National Sales Manager in a FORTUNE 100 company in just eight short years, I found Roger's expertise crucial to my success. Our company actively seeks out Roger's applicants. They are the best of the best. If you want to know how business works and what savvy business people look for in a military officer, and if you want to discover the tactics and strategies to conquer the interviewer, this book is for you."

    — *Frank Pichichero*
       National Sales Manager
       American Hydro-Surgical Instruments

"The military officer possesses the winning combination of developed leadership skills and a focus on achievement. The difficult part is in properly marketing these strengths to civilian industry. Roger Cameron is the definitive authority on the subject. His expertise is unmatched and an invaluable resource for military officers transitioning to Corporate America. Roger provides a direct, honest, and concise guide to the preparation and interviewing process. Arm yourself for continuing success with **PCS**!"

    — *Don Patchell*
       Research Project Manager
       Hallmark Cards, Inc.

"**PCS to Corporate America** and my association with Roger Cameron marked the turning point in my professional career. **PCS** prepared me for a move from the ordinary to a dream job and career. Many have asked how I managed to land such a great job right out of the military. The answer: **PCS** laid the groundwork and taught me to control my environment."

    — *Beth Gulitus*
       Sales Representative
       Ethicon Endo-Surgery, Division of Johnson & Johnson

"Recipe for Success: 1 cup military leadership training, 1 cup common sense, 2 cups Roger Cameron. Mix well. Season liberally with Purpose. Watch carefully while the offers rise. (Yield: Success!) Clear and concise, Roger cuts through the fat, leaving behind all of the essentials any job applicant should know. Though geared specifically for the military officer, PCS should be required reading for anyone who wishes to make a job change."
> — Katherine Winterbauer
> Design Engineer
> Thomson Consumer Electronics

"A must-read book for any officer leaving the service. Roger is simply the best in the business. Throw away all the other books. Read, digest, and listen to what he has to say and you will be well-prepared to enter the corporate interviewing gauntlet!"
> — Kyle MacGibbon
> Product Manager
> Abbott Diagnostics

"To this day, I remember and live by Roger's guidance which outlined the three key elements necessary to be successful in sales: 1) Be honest, 2) Be sincere, and 3) Always have the customer's best interest in mind. Roger's wisdom and guidance have helped shape my career and, in turn, the careers with which I have been entrusted."
> — Tony Westbrook
> Director of Marketing
> Dopaco, Inc.

"This book comes to you from the George S. Patton of Corporate Recruiters. Roger is tough, holds the highest standards, and leads the people on his team to a win every time. Be thankful to have your own copy of his guide to success. When you have read it twice, read it again!"
> — Adam Lobert
> Senior Drilling Supervisor
> Mobil Oil Corporation

"If you are leaving the military for Corporate America, read Roger's book! Roger has set a standard for preparing Junior Military Officers to enter the business world that no one else has come close to matching."
> — David Edmonds
> Human Resources Manager
> Pepsi-Cola

"Roger's knowledge, dedication, and experience are unparalleled in recruiting and have been passed on in this book. It should be required reading when leaving the military and entering industry. Our company has never regretted the decision to hire exclusively through Roger."
> — Mike Teague
> President
> Walter Lorenz Surgical, Inc.

"In the Army, I trained hard every day to be prepared for any mission. But I must tell you that I have never felt as thoroughly prepared for anything as I was for the interviewing process after completing Roger's program. All the helpful interviewing techniques continue to pay dividends today in my sales work. Roger's book should be required reading as part of the military out-processing checklist!"
— *Mike Marmaro*
Key Account Manager
Airco Gases, Division of BOC

"There is none better! Preparation and presentation are essentials for a successful interview. In his book, Roger captures and gives to his readers the arts and skills needed to sell oneself as number one. Read this book and join Corporate America!"
— *Dave Hernandez*
Regional Manager
Ethicon Endo-Surgery, Division of Johnson & Johnson

"PCS to Corporate America was, without a doubt, the most valuable tool I utilized during my career search. Roger provides practical, no-nonsense information on every page. If you want the truth about what it takes to make a successful transition to Corporate America, there is no substitute for PCS."
— *Andrew Finn*
Sales Representative
J.T. Baker, Inc.

"PCS provides a detailed road map to guide a Junior Officer's hard work and leadership experience into Corporate America. PCS will transform nervous energy into a successful, confident interview style."
— *Tim Papa*
Operations Leader
International Paper

"Roger made my transition into Corporate America a very memorable experience. In PCS, he stresses the importance of preparation and knowing yourself. I came to believe in myself and what I had to offer the corporate world. Take Roger's words to heart and the interviewing process will become a great experience!"
— *Jenni Jones*
Area Manager
Pizza Hut, Inc., Division of PepsiCo

"PCS is the most valuable book of its kind on the market, and a must read for all JMOs headed to Corporate America!"
— *Kent Williams*
Regional Sales Manager
Walter Lorenz Surgical, Inc.

"Read **PCS**. Learn the power of preparation — your competition for that great job already knows it. With the help of **PCS**, I was able to channel my drive into productive preparation."
> — Matt Stone
> Assistant Account Executive
> Leo Burnett

"Roger tackles an important and complex subject matter and provides a nuts and bolts approach that will dramatically increase your odds of accomplishing your end goal, a job offer. When it comes to military recruiting, Roger is the authority. Read his book, follow his guidance and practice what he tells you and you will be successful in transitioning into Corporate America."
> — Steven Butler
> Manager of Recruitment
> Wal-Mart Stores, Inc.

"Having been trained as a Navy pilot, I had become accustomed to high performance. Roger's professionalism and commitment have been top notch! I knew this first as the candidate, later as the client, and for 22 years as a confidant."
> — Don Carpenter
> Director, National Accounts
> Honeywell

"Every military officer leaving the military should read this book! Roger's knowledge and experience teaching military officers how to break into the corporate fast track is unparalleled."
> — Scott Relf
> Director of Marketing
> E&J Gallo Winery

"SIERRA HOTEL! Roger has condensed 27+ years of experience into a wonderfully compact book. Read, apply, and succeed. This book is a must for any military officer!"
> — Asima "Sam" Syed
> Vice President – Marketing
> Genesco

"Roger's expertise in preparing Junior Military Officers for successful transitions from the military to Corporate America is unparalleled. His techniques for interview preparation should be 'cast in gold' and adhered to by all transitioning JMOs. As a former Army officer who recently made the transition, I relied 100% on the guidance provided by Roger, **PCS To Corporate America**, and the rest of the Cameron-Brooks Team. Roger is the best, so don't transition without this book!"
> — Ken Keller
> Senior Systems Developer
> Burlington Northern Railroad Company

"Roger helped me with my interviewing skills, but more importantly, he gave me valuable insights into the business world. With these insights, plus a lot of hard work, I have assumed additional responsibilities in the corporate world. We continue to use Roger's candidates to meet our sales force needs across the country. I'm proud to have been associated with Roger all these years. Read PCS and gain the insights that can help you, too."

> — *Bill Quilici*
> *Regional Manager*
> *Ethicon Suture, Division of Johnson & Johnson*

"Roger's attention to detail is only exceeded by the service he provides for both the applicant and the hiring corporation."

> — *Rick Bifulco*
> *Manager of National Accounts*
> *Mobil Chemical Company*

"It is not enough to be a top-notch officer — you must be able to effectively communicate why you've been able to 'make it happen'! Roger will teach you everything you need to successfully get onto the 'Corporate Fast Track'. Roger knows what it takes to be successful in the corporate world."

> — *Christine Henry*
> *Compliance Coordinator*
> *Airco Gases, Division of BOC*

"Buy this book and trust Roger. He's got his facts straight and he will keep your eyes on the prize — a rewarding career."

> — *Walt Horstman*
> *Vice President*
> *American Savings Bank*

"Fifteen years ago, Roger did an outstanding job of matching my experience and my expectations with my current employer. Today, I count on him to provide top-notch managers for my organization. With his degree of understanding, he is unsurpassed in the recruiting field in meeting the needs of both candidates and corporations. Roger selects the best and prepares them the best!"

> — *Larry Chaplin*
> *Director of Maintenance*
> *Schneider National, Inc.*

"I have known Roger for 16 years. His assistance was critical to starting me on a very successful career. No wonder PCS is a best seller."

> — *Thomas Blackburn*
> *President*
> *Chesapeake Paper Products Company*

"It's amazing — men and women who would never think about going into battle unprepared do just that when they begin their search for a job in Corporate America. They begin their interview process unfocused and without the ability to articulate their skills in an interview setting. Roger's training pushes military officers to focus, articulate, and fight for the best career possible. I couldn't have been matched so perfectly with my current top-notch company without Roger and **PCS**."

> — *Randy Aguero*
> *Medical Representative*
> *Ciba-Geigy Corporation*

"Roger is on the money with his strategy and advice for establishing a career in Corporate America. Perhaps his most incisive observation of Corporate America is that recruiters need to be convinced of a candidate's commitment to making the transition from the military. Not only do Roger and his team help you translate military experience into sought-after skills, but they also help you articulate your commitment to a new career. I am convinced that this competitive edge was decisive in my getting precisely the position I was seeking."

> — *Moira Williams*
> *Consultant*
> *KPMG Peat Marwick*

"Roger Cameron's coaching, seminars, and writings helped me learn more about myself, and how my military experience set me apart from my peers in Corporate America. With this knowledge, I learned and developed an interviewing style that demonstrated confidence and emphasized my strongest qualities. My interviewing abilities helped me begin a career with my first choice of companies and gain acceptance to my first choice of business schools. These abilities also helped me transition from engineering to sales to corporate recruiting. I frequently refer to the lessons that Roger has written in **PCS**. I continue to find them invaluable."

> — *Peter Miller*
> *Sales Engineer*
> *Airco Gases, Division of BOC*

"Luck is being prepared when opportunity knocks. The key to a successful transition from the military into Corporate America is a direct result of thorough preparation. Roger Cameron operates within this spirit to ensure you are provided the best opportunity. This, and more, is captured in **PCS**. Read it and take the first steps to becoming the luckiest person to 'PCS into Corporate America.'"

> — *David Harris, Jr.*
> *Sales Development Manager*
> *Ethicon Suture, Division of Johnson & Johnson*

PCS TO CORPORATE AMERICA

From Military Tactics To Corporate Interviewing Strategy

ROGER CAMERON

Odenwald Press
Dallas

PCS TO CORPORATE AMERICA
From Military Tactics To Corporate Interviewing Strategy

Copyright © 1990 Roger Cameron
Second edition 1994

Cover design by Ellen Fountain/Fountain Graphics

Published by Odenwald Press, Dallas, Texas

Library of Congress Cataloging in Publication Data

Cameron, Roger, 1935-
     PCS to corporate America: from military tactics to
     corporate interviewing strategy / Roger Cameron
     Includes index.
     ISBN 0-9623216-5-6 : $19.95
1. Employment interviewing. 2. Retired military personnel —
Vocational guidance. 3. Retired military personnel —
Employment. I. Title.
HF5549.5.I6C35   1994   92-21911
650.14'024355—dc20   CIP

Printed in the United States of America

CONTENTS

Letter to Military Officers

ACKNOWLEDGMENTS

I sincerely want to give a warm thank you to three key members of our Cameron-Brooks Team — René Brooks, Mary Lou White, and Leslie Klonoff — who have been "cornerstones" for the writing of my books. Each has traveled thousands of miles with me during their careers, offering quality insight and advice. It would have been impossible to experience all my success without them.

To my friends, business associates, clients, and Cameron-Brooks alumni around the world who continually encourage and support me, a special thank you and appreciation. I have had the best job in America these past 27 years, having the opportunity to interact with so many exceptional people.

Those of you who have written words of praise as readers of *PCS* deserve a special acknowledgment. It has been inspirational to hear from thousands whose lives have been positively impacted as a result of this book.

Thanks also to Sylvia Odenwald, my editor and publisher, who continually told me how "great" the book was. Now, based on growing demand, the second edition, and readers' comments and successes, I believe her!

And, finally, thank you to Corporate America for believing in the quality of our military officers.

How To Gain The Most From This Book!

Hopefully, you are reading *PCS* long before you make your transition. While it is valuable at all times, its value is enhanced the earlier you read it.

I often talk with officers who share with me the value that *PCS* has brought to their successful career searches. Without fail, each of these officers recounts a systematic approach to reading the book along with specific points that enabled them to retain and apply what they learned. I want to suggest 3 steps to assure you, too, gain the most from *PCS*.

First   Take a long evening and read *PCS* cover-to-cover. Do not stop to do the recommended exercises. It is important to first understand all the points the book covers and the significance given to different issues.

Second   Slowly reread *PCS* with the following supplies in hand:
- <u>Three highlighters of different colors</u>
  Determine your own code for highlighting issues of different intensity of importance.
- <u>Small post-it notes</u>
  Write key points to flag pages and signal points of significance.
- <u>Varied colored pens</u>
  Mark it up! Write in the columns, make special remarks relative to your development.

Third   Now, read the book again and practice all exercises using a tape recorder and notebook for additional reference. Evaluate each exercise, listen to the tapes with others whose judgment and constructive feedback will be of benefit. Take advantage of all material in the book, especially the valuable exercises and information in the Appendix.
Practice, Practice, Practice!

PCS will become one of the most important books in your library. As your career progresses and you interview for promotion, do not assume that you will automatically recall your interviewing techniques. Reread *PCS*. As you gain the responsibility of interviewing and hiring for your company, and are required to identify individuals and recommend them for hire, your credibility is on the line. Reread *PCS*. Utilize *PCS* long term and make it your primary career resource.

Most importantly, never loan your copy of *PCS* to anyone. I promise, you won't get it back. The value of your remarks and references represents an extensive amount of dedicated time, along with important development notes that will make a difference in your career.

Give your friends who want to borrow *PCS* our toll free number (1-800-222-9235). We'll have *PCS* in their hands via priority mail in 2 days!

FOREWORD

For years, I said I would never write a book. Unfortunately, the interviewing world is a very dynamic world — a world of constant change with constant evaluation of better methods of identifying and selecting employees. Because our applicants were coming to the marketplace with more and more questions that needed to be answered, I decided a book that addressed these questions was needed. My hope is that this book will continue to bring my applicants and other military officers to the marketplace better prepared.

You may have noticed that this is the second edition of *PCS*. While I have received nothing but outstanding comments on the first edition, I did find that some points could be clarified and that new issues should be discussed. Therefore, I feel confident that this updated edition includes enhancements beneficial to your success in interviewing. As always, you must take **action** to gain the full benefit of this book.

I've attempted to keep the "fluff" out of this book and to bring it quickly to the bottom line. I know that the majority of you (military officers) are extremely busy holding down a full-time job that takes 10 to 14 hours of your day and, unfortunately, many weekends, too. So, I felt it best to write a book you could get into immediately, one that focuses on what you need to do to be successful in interviewing. I'm confident this book will do exactly that.

I have not talked about the things that you, as a military officer, do so well. Many things are so innate to you that I don't need to discuss them. I have taken military officers through my interviewing procedure lectures many times, and frequently they have come away feeling as if they will never do anything right. I always point out that I am talking only about the things they find difficult rather than those they do correctly. For you to pick up a book and read about things that come naturally to you would be a waste of your time and mine. It is more important for me to talk about the things that you have a tendency to miss or to do incorrectly. While some suggestions may seem to be demeaning, I assure you they are not. I am very proud to be known as one of the originators of the process that gets military officers successfully into Corporate America. In no way do I intend to be demeaning. I feel strongly that I cannot allow some minor things in an interview to eliminate you when I could have mentioned them. No book can cover every situation for every individual.

Throughout this book, I recommend ways of analyzing specific questions. Only a weak person would read a book and repeat the verbiage word for word. You must take your thoughts and develop your own answers. Be yourself. If you allow a company to hire you while hiding behind a facade, it won't work. Ultimately, the company will look at you and wonder why they hired you. Make sure that a company hires you for what and who you are, not what you can pretend to be during a series of interviews.

Psychologically, there are three selves — you at your best, you at your average, and you at your worst. Obviously, in an interviewing situation, you must be at your best. Companies expect you to interview at 100%. That is the only percentage that will get your hired.

How do you get to be your best? Preparation. I have had companies say, "Roger, if applicants won't work hard to accomplish one of their own objectives (a great career), why should we assume that they will work hard to accomplish objectives that we give them?" I have to agree. Amazingly, some applicants will come to the marketplace assuming success without preparation. (That would be like you telling me that you are going through an annual inspection on Monday morning and that you started preparation for the inspection on Friday.) You know what will happen. You will fail. You may say, "We should be natural interviewees." That just isn't what life's all about. You have to prepare for the tough objectives. And, as you know, the harder you prepare, the more successful you are.

You learned this in grade school: The harder you worked to learn, the easier the exams became and the higher your grade point average. Everything in life is based on preparation. Not one of us is natural at everything we do.

You must read this book with a positive attitude. Say to yourself, "I'm going to listen to an individual who has recruited military officers and helped place them in Corporate America for over 27 years."

I will put my success for placing applicants with Corporate America against any other recruiting firm or recruiter in America. I have listened to what companies are looking for, and I have seen the kind of individuals they are hiring. I have seen the individuals who have gone to the top of Corporate America. I have noticed the pattern. It has been a pattern created from day one — the pattern of preparation — of people who do their work thoroughly. It is interesting to watch those applicants I bring to Corporate America. Early in the process, they build their resumes, read their books, and start working on the difficult questions. It seems the better the applicants are, the earlier they start their preparation. They are not procrastinators.

I have also noticed that the patterns some people establish for themselves are not successful patterns. They assume that they can simply verbalize the answers in a matter of seconds. However, they are not quite able to juggle all of the balls. They can't **quite** make it happen. As long as they have an excuse, they feel that they're allowed to fail. Some of those excuses include the following: "I'm sorry I didn't get it done; I was in the field." "I'm sorry I didn't get it done; I've had to work 14-hour days." "I'm sorry I didn't get it done, but I had to go TDY," or "I had an ORSE." This type of applicant is not what Corporate America is paying me to recruit. Corporations want people who do the following:

- Control their environment.
- Effectively use their time.
- Are extremely well-organized.
- Know exactly what needs to be done, when it needs to be done, and get it done.

I am frequently asked, "What is the bottom line, Roger? What is Corporate America looking for in development candidates?" This is a good question, and there's an easy answer. They're looking for individuals who can get things done in spite of the difficulties that arise — **make-it-happen, goal-oriented, mission-oriented types**.

My acceptance rate of the officers who I have interviewed over the years is 12 percent. Often, they say, "Roger Cameron is tough." No, Roger Cameron is not tough. It's just that I know who Corporate America is paying me to recruit. There are people who are probably very good performers who are not going to be hired because of their inability to communicate. What is more important than the ability to communicate, to persuade, and to get your peers, superiors, subordinates, customers, and competition to see your point of view through the art of communication? People say, "Roger, if they would hire me, they would see that I'm a good performer." Sometimes, I feel the same way. If they would just hire some military officers, they would discover how great they are. Unfortunately, recruiting just doesn't work that way.

As I have written and edited this book, I've noticed that it comes across hard-nosed and bottom line. But, that's pretty much the way Corporate America thinks. I have watched companies rule out people I felt were very capable. In fact, I knew they were good because I had their performance evaluations, but, because they did not have the ability to communicate their successes, top companies walked away from them.

I am often asked how I could stay in this business for over 27 years. I always give the same answer. In all these years, I've had thousands of jobs presented to me. I have never seen a job that interested me enough to even take more than a casual look at it. I'm not so sure that there is a more exciting business than that of recruiting young men and women for top development positions in some of the top companies in Corporate America. It's been exciting to watch these young men and women move up the corporate ladder, have their successes, and become key employees within their companies. I have received thousands of letters of appreciation over the years, and every one of them made me feel good. They made me realize how lucky I am to be in this business.

I talk to and hear from people I placed — 15 years ago, 17 years ago, 20 years ago — who are still using many of the techniques my staff and I taught them. Those applicants have made me proud. Each time I recruit an individual for Corporate America, I ask myself the question, "Do I want to put my name beside this individual as he or she comes to industry?" That's important to me. I want to be proud of each recruit I place in industry. And, of the overwhelming majority, I can be. I've had very few failures over the years.

I feel that many comments in this book will allow you to interview for any type of job with any type of organization. I would like to put my plug in for the profit-oriented world, the world of capitalism. It is a world that is exciting and challenging. When I think of how young America is, I realize that our greatness is based on the industrial nature of the United States. We have been leaders in so many areas for many years. Sure it's true that some countries have copied products we have originated and made them better because of circumstances in their countries, such as cheaper labor. But, I'll still put America against anyone else. I'll still put our engineers, our finance people, and our data processing people up against anyone in the world.

Working with the kinds of companies I have represented over the years is still very exciting. I have companies today who have a 20% growth factor, even 40% growth factor in a year, and some of them even more. When you take a highly sophisticated company that has that kind of growth, you have to have outstanding people to accomplish and manage it. The military officers whom I've brought into Corporate America have loved the fact that they are not practicing, but are, in fact, doing. What they learn (on a daily basis), they can apply. When they go home at night, they can measure the fact that their company has been able to take a step closer to its objective. It's satisfying to be in an environment where you know you must constantly be changing and improving, and where you're working with positive-minded people, people who come to work in the morning because they **want** to be there, who are excited about what their company does and what their products can do for mankind, people who feel it is exciting to be paid and promoted according to their performance.

Recruiting the military officer for Corporate America has always been interesting. I can't say it has always been fun. I remember when I helped originate this business, I talked to companies about why they should hire the military officer. I also remember some of their comments: "Excuse me, Roger, you're suggesting that we should hire somebody who operates in the world of nonprofit, in the world of appropriation instead of the world of profitability? Roger, what are we supposed to do with this individual who, for the last five years, has been involved with tanks, guns and artillery, airplanes, and ships? I'm a little confused as to why we should hire this person. We should hire someone who is proud that he/she spends all of the budget? As a matter of fact, they even put it on their resumes."

That's the way things were when this military recruiting industry started. It's grown interestingly over the years — grown to the point where today military officers have demonstrated their value to Corporate America. Today, we can point to military officers who are presidents of some of the top companies in Corporate America. Suddenly, companies which have been cynics over the years about military officers are starting to take a very hard look at them. Finally, companies are calling us rather than our calling them.

You've been good. As a matter of fact, you've been great! I don't know of any individuals who have had more impact than military officers coming into Corporate America. We admit to you that we made a lot of mistakes over the years in evaluating military personnel, but today we know you very well. We know what makes you successful and what your weaknesses are as you leave the military. We have developed programs that will bring you up to speed quickly in areas where you need more development. We know where to go to find a particular background. We know what you need to do in the military to make yourself successful in Corporate America. Today, we know the kind of private lifestyle you need to have for success in industry. You were an unknown when we started this business. It has been fun to watch our applicants' progress, yet agonizing to observe some of their failures. Fortunately, today these failures are at a minimum in relation to what they were when we first started recruiting military officers.

I often interview those officers I have brought to Corporate America over the years (after they've been in industry) and ask what, if anything, they feel they have gained or lost by moving into industry. Usually, I receive three positive answers and one negative answer.

The three positives we hear have never changed. The first positive is the quality of life — the ability to tell your sons or daughters that you're going to be at Little League at 6:00 P.M. They just know you're going to be there. You tell your family that you'll be home for dinner, and they know you will be there. You know that evenings and weekends are yours. You can establish a vacation date six months down the road and know that you will be there. I have rarely seen a vacation ever being canceled by a company in all the years I've been associated with Corporate America.

The second positive relates to the input into your career. It's true. Companies ask you, "What is it you want to do? What kind of positions will enhance your career? What do you expect your company to do to ensure that you have a successful career?" You have a lot of input — veto rights for locations, positions, and the timing of promotions.

Third, our applicants have told us that their net worth has significantly increased. Why? Because most people in America create the bulk of their net worth through equity built up in their homes. Unfortunately, when military officers PCS, they spend most of their equity on the sale of the house, the purchase of the new house, and relocation expenses over and above what the military is willing to pay. In Corporate America, most industries pay every cent of that relocation, and your equity remains in your pocket. We get many other positive comments, but these three comments are the most significant in encouraging officers to move into Corporate America.

The one negative is that they feel they do not immediately enjoy the same degree of camaraderie in corporate life that they enjoyed in the military. At first, we received this answer from military officers and their spouses. Today, we get it only from some spouses. As military officers come into a company, usually ex-officers are there to greet them on the first day. So, for the officer today, that transition into Corporate America is easy and comfortable. The spouse still goes into the neighborhood where each neighbor comes from a unique background. They don't all have the same problems, or the same lifestyle. They are not all going off to a social event together or going on a European assignment, etc. However, we're finding spouses commenting on this less and less as we get dual family careers where the spouse is also going to work for a company and, therefore, having his or her own career involvement. We have also stolen an idea from the military. Many of our companies are now providing sponsors who will introduce you to the neighborhood and the community.

As I've always said to military officers, it's not that one environment is good and the other environment is bad. They are different. Some of you will determine that the military is better for you than Corporate America. We understand that. We like to think that as some of you read this book, you will feel that Corporate America is where you want to have your career. For those of you who choose Corporate America, here's a word of caution. Do not feel that Corporate America is going to be a cure-all for the problems that you might have in the military. We have our problems. Some of the things we do are not always smart. Corporate America is affected by economic conditions, as is the military.

There is no ideal company, job, or environment. However, I feel it is critically important that you come to Corporate America as an individual who intends to go to work for a great company and to stay with that company. I am a very strong advocate of conducting a proper analysis and determining with which company you want to have your career. I do not encourage moving constantly from one company to another. Sometime during the course of your career, you are going to have some personal challenges arise that will tend to divert you from your job. This situation will cause you to focus on your family. You want to know that your company will support you during these difficult times.

Too many times, applicants will move from Company A to Company B to simply find greater difficulties with Company B. If you expect the company to remain with you during the difficult times of your life, it is only fair that you stay with the company during any difficulties they have. Many employees want to change companies when they see a product lose market share. It's okay for the company to support them during **their** difficult times, but they don't want to support their company during the **company's** difficult times. That's not fair. I encourage you to be loyal. Jumping from one company to another does not always advance your career. All you have really done is change the problems. Every time you make a move, it is difficult for you and your family emotionally, and it tells many things about you that you would not want said.

I hope you will find this book an aid in interviewing. Any time you have a question on an issue discussed in the book, feel free to give me a call. I wish that a book could cover everything, but I know it can't. It's similar to the preparation prior to our Career Conferences. We try to answer every question we think an applicant may encounter in an interview, but, after years of experience, I have found corporate recruiters can still surprise me. I think you will find the major issues for military officers are covered in this book. Have fun reading it, and the best of luck to you in your career search.

STOP! STOP! STOP!
DON'T READ ANY MORE
OF THIS BOOK WITHOUT
A HIGHLIGHTER.

Use a highlighter to emphasize those issues that are important to you. As a matter of fact, all your interviewing preparation should be done with a highlighter and note pad in hand! Don't hesitate to write notes to yourself in the borders of each page so that you can quickly refresh your memory and flip back through the book.

PCS should be used as a career reference book. Never, throughout your career, should it be out of arm's length. Do not loan this or any other reference book from your library. Every quality book must be read, referred to, and reread. There are some books I reread every year to remind me of valuable points.

CHAPTER 1

The Evaluation Process

"Companies like mine will hurry to read Roger's book to figure out how we can better attract talented military officers before the best young officers have all been hired by our competitors! Officers will read the book because it will stand at attention among a dismal company of ineffective 'how to' guides that never before could give them exactly what they needed. Not everyone has the privilege of personally working with Roger. Now, every officer can benefit from Roger's many years of successfully finding and shaping present and future leadership of the business community."
— Bill Watkins
Veit, Inc.

CHAPTER 1

The Evaluation Process

Early Recruiting Days
Corporate America initially believed that the military officer would have a difficult time being competitive in the corporate world as a development candidate. There were three basic reasons for this. When I first started recruiting the military officer, most were leaving the military five to seven years after their age group graduated from college and entered the world of profit. That meant they spent five to seven years in the nonprofit world (the military) and were then entering the world of profitability. How could they logically catch up with their age group in minimum time?

I compare this situation to running a race with recent college graduates. You had to finish in the top 10% of those who ran the race to be considered a winner. No problem, you say. But, when you get to the track and you're in the blocks, I reach down to tap you (the military officer) on the shoulder and I say, "By the way, when I pull the trigger, you stay at the blocks. You wait until all the college graduates in your age group get a fifth of the way around the track. Then you may start." Undoubtedly, you would stand up and say, "Come on, Roger, that's not realistic." So, you see, objectively speaking, it made sense that you, the military officer, would have a hard time catching up with your age group as you entered Corporate America. You notice that I said **age** group, not **year** group. In the military, all you need to do is be concerned about being competitive with your **year** group. When you come into Corporate America, you aren't measured by a year group, only by an **age** group.

As I examined the bulk of officers coming out, I discovered that well over 90% had never used their education as it was designed to be used. So, that was a second strike against them. Education in Corporate America is a **tool**, not a ticket.

In those days, the third point was an economic factor — forced retirement at a mandatory age. Consequently, Corporate America had to retire those military officers and give them the same benefits even though they had worked five to seven years less than those college graduates. These were three major factors why companies had much less interest in the officer as a development candidate.

Post-Vietnam Recruiting

What forced recruiters to rethink this situation? The Vietnam War. Recruiters discovered that when they went to the college campus to hire development candidates, there weren't enough students due to the draft. So, suddenly, recruiters had to reevaluate and reassess the military officer. Corporations started hiring military officers — reluctantly. They objectively felt you would have a hard time competing with your age group. But, as Corporate America measured you against the very best from the college campus, they discovered you were catching up in very little time.

What were the factors causing you to close the gap so quickly? When Corporate America analyzed your performance, they found many **subjective** benefits from your military experience. This became an exciting discovery for industry. All of a sudden, Corporate America had **two** supply sources for hiring development candidates — the college campus and the military. They also discovered that the military officer was a very inexpensive hire compared to the recent college recruit.

When corporate recruiters say "yes" to an applicant, they indicate intent to bring that person into their headquarters for follow-up interviews. The average cost for one of these trips is $3,000. With college graduates, only 30% of those brought in are good enough to get an offer. And, the offer acceptance rate is 25%. It actually takes **13** college graduates flown into headquarters to get one hire. That's $39,000 in recruiting expenses! With military officers, recruiters are getting 90% offered and accepted, meaning that even after paying a recruiting firm's $8,000 to $10,000 fee, they still save significant dollars. And, Uncle Sam will move the officer to the corporation. With a college student, the company incurs that expense.

Over the years, interest, enthusiasm, and excitement for the military officer have grown. One problem, though, is that no one knows how many officers are coming out of the military in a year. Recruiters would love for Congress, the Army, Air Force, Navy, and Marine Corps to get together to determine exactly how many officers are going to leave the military in a year and what their qualifications will be. Sadly, that's still an unknown. Therefore, Corporate America must fill the majority of employment needs with college graduates. With college students, statistics reveal exactly how many are graduating, what degree and GPA they will have, how many are going on to graduate school, how many will work for their parents, and how many will travel for a couple of years or move into Corporate America. Companies can monitor their progress toward graduation. With officers, there may be 150 available, or there may be 650.

The enthusiasm for the military officer has grown over the years. Today, rather than talking about subjective successes, I can point my finger to officers who have been highly successful as military officers and who have gone to the top of major corporations. Today, more and more companies are eager to hire you and benefit from your ability to make things happen.

Training

As you are brought into Corporate America, you are expected to perform immediately. Applicants often say, "Roger, could you tell me how industry is going to train me?" If you have the word "training" in your vocabulary, throw it in the garbage can. Take it out in the middle of your driveway and run over it. Put it in the middle of the freeway so hundreds of cars will drive over it. Don't ask Corporate America about its training program.

Corporations basically say, "We train college graduates. We don't train the military officer." You should have received your training in the military and should bring that training to Corporate America. There's no reason why you shouldn't be able to have an impact on profitability instantly. You've learned how to accomplish difficult objectives. You've learned how to prioritize, organize, and effectively manage time, to break tough objectives down into component parts, and to motivate subordinates to help accomplish those objectives. Whether you're applying your expertise to solve a problem in the military world or a problem in the world of profitability, the methods are the same.

Is there an exception to the rule? Absolutely. If the company brings up the word "training" either in their literature or in the interview itself, then you may explore the training further. Even then, I would be careful. You need to suggest that, as a military officer, you can have an immediate impact. Industry will pay you more than a recent college graduate. You will expect to be promoted faster than a recent college graduate. Be careful of this word "training." I often say training is synonymous with a very nasty four-letter word. That four-letter word is "cost." So, if we put the word "cost" in the place of training, look what your question to Corporate America is. "What money will you invest to help me perform difficult objectives?"

Corporations may have to give you some orientation to a new world, but orientation is significantly different from training. Orientation is basically what you in the military consider "on the job training." At the same time you're performing, you are also learning.

After all, if you're going to catch up with your age group, you'll want to get in and get started immediately. The less time you take to become competitive, the more quickly you can move ahead of your age group into significant management roles.

The Development Manager
American industry has a three-fold labor force. First, there is the blue collar laborer who is either union or non-union. Then, there are two layers of management — exactly like the Service. There is the non-development manager (you call them warrant officers) and then the development manager (who is the equivalent of the commissioned officer).

A non-development manager is a person who develops a specific area of expertise. These managers are really not targeted to go to the top 10% of Corporate America. It's not that they can't do so, but their goal is to develop a special area or skill. The military equivalent of the non-development manager is the warrant officer who becomes an expert pilot or whose expertise is in personnel, data processing, finance, or maintenance.

The development candidate is a generalist. He or she has an absolute burning desire to move to the top 10% of Corporate

America and has the perceived ability to accomplish that objective. It is important that you understand (as you come into industry) how you, as a commissioned officer, fit into a major corporation. As a development candidate for Corporate America, a lot of time, money, expertise, and effort will be spent in getting you to the point where you can have a major impact on the direction of your company.

This is not an overnight venture any more than it is in the military. Moving from LTJG through LT to LCDR and on up the chain of command takes time. There are many things you need to learn and experiences you must have to become a top manager. So, it is important to realize that these steps are necessary, and it takes time to happen. Don't come to Corporate America feeling that you will be an overnight sensation.

Development candidates must be "growable people" — young men and women who are constantly reading and expanding their knowledge base, not only about their job, but also outside their job area. Corporate America is looking for people who have diverse interests with the ability to prioritize those interests and use that knowledge in a timely fashion on the job.

Last year in my travels around the world (looking for development candidates for my company clients), I interviewed exactly 2,125 officers from the Army, Navy, Air Force, and Marine Corps. Out of the 2,125, I accepted exactly 246 and brought them to the marketplace. What makes me consistently accept only 11% to 12% of the applicants I interview? Let's look at this evaluation process.

Three Categories Of Your Life
Many applicants fail because, in the interview, they focus only on their military training. If you had the ability to see the

commonalities within the profile of the top 10% of management in Corporate America, you would find that those commonalities reach all the way back to high school. If you come to an interview talking only about what you have done in the military, you're attempting to stand on one of three legs. Good luck! In a "down market," luck isn't going to do you any good.

We evaluate your high school, college, and military careers and look **equally** at the factors in the three different categories. **"Equally"** is the key word. First, we evaluate high school records on quantifiable factors: the grade point average, the size of your class, and your ranking within that class. That narrows down your performance factor compared to other students' performance. We look at the difficulty factor of the curriculum. Was it an honors program? Then, we look at extracurricular activities. What did you do outside academics? In the extracurricular activities, our most important question is this: "Were you elected to leadership roles by your peers or superiors? What contribution did you make?" We would also like to see the beginning of a positive work ethic.

After looking at your high school accomplishments, we evaluate your college years. We cover the same areas and questions used in evaluating high school information, but we add two critical factors — the known quality of your college and the known quality of your curriculum.

What is the first thing we look for in the military? The positions you've held. In your particular branch, were these positions career enhancing? Did you get them at the right time? Did you hold them for the right length of time? We then proceed to your officer evaluations. We look for impact statements — statements which lift you above your contemporaries. Each of you knows (in the different branches of the military) the inflation factor. So do we. We know every nuance, every idiosyncrasy of individual statements made in your officer evaluations.

Then, we look at what you have done outside the military. This is the conversational portion of the interview. We start with poise and self-confidence. This is important because you will be placed in a new environment and be expected to have an impact on profitability immediately. You must have the poise and confidence to move into an unknown situation and perform quickly. While it is true that most of this is subjective in the interview, we can determine it by the following:

1) your ease or ability to persuasively communicate;
2) your ability to use first names;
3) your ability to develop instant rapport and understand the corporate world.

You must communicate persuasively in order to have impact in as short a period of time as possible. Show us you effectively use time. There are many ways to make that determination even though, for the most part, it is a subjective evaluation. Finally, we look for a person who is constantly striving to grow.

Sometimes, when we evaluate an officer's high school and college experience, we find extremely outstanding credentials from high school. We ask ourselves, "How did they get it all done?" However, when we get to the military, we discover they do **nothing** but their job. We don't see the growth outside the job. The military encourages you to design your life around your job. We're not saying the military is wrong in that. We're simply saying that's not what we're looking for in Corporate America. We seek individuals who have continued to develop their family interest, extracurricular activities, and life outside the military.

When we first began recruiting officers, we discovered a heavy turnover rate within a two- to three-year period of time. Officers were telling us they were just not getting the job challenge in Corporate America that they were getting in the military. This didn't make any sense to us. We didn't get that from recent college graduates or from experienced employees. We got it only from military officers. Then, we discovered what was happening. The officers were working 12- and 14-hour days in the military (sometimes Saturday and Sunday) week after week. When they came to Corporate America, they were putting in eight- and nine-hour days. They expected their jobs in Corporate America to fill up their lives as their jobs in the military had. They **didn't**. And they **won't**. Corporate America is **not** going to take control of your outside life.

Today, we look for people who have developed outside interests, and we don't really care what they are. We don't care whether it's running, hiking, handball, family outings, reading, flying, boating, camping, Boy Scouts, Girl Scouts, or Big Brothers/Big Sisters. We like to see a diversity of activities. We're not looking for carbon copies. We want to see people who are involved — people who are growing.

We are also interested in the fact that if you're married, you have a good marriage — if you have a family, that you have a good family life. But, after all, these are illegal interview questions. We can't ask you to answer them. However, if there are things about you we don't know, our choice is to walk away and proceed to someone else who gives us the kind of information we need to make a decision. So, if you're talking about your extracurricular activities, include your spouse and children. Be honest with us. Tell us what you do. Don't create an answer for us. **Don't tell us what you think we want to hear**. Tell it the way it is. You must give us information in all aspects of your life. You must be comfortable with yourself as an individual as well as with your ability to perform.

Corporate America cannot mandate that people work well with others. They can get up and walk out the door any time they want. So, it is important for us to hire people with professional quality — people who work well with others and who are eager to come to work each morning. We're not looking for the cocky person whose self-confidence controls them. We want people who have total control of their self-confidence. They don't have to wear it on their sleeve. They know they're good. They don't have to act as if they're the best. As I interview around the world, it's interesting to find that the really good people do not have to inflate the numbers. They are not afraid to tell me that on a scale of 1-10, they're a 7 in leadership style, they're an 8 in computer science, or that they're a 5 and lack "hands-on" mechanical experience. Only those who lack self-confidence feel they must tell me they're a 10 in everything they do. We want people who have good self-insight — people who feel comfortable with themselves. They can honestly identify their strengths and weaknesses. People want a company to hire them on the basis of what they are, not what they can pretend to be in an interview or in a series of interviews.

Do we always get the ideal candidate? In all my years of recruiting, I probably never have. We take an individual and put the positives on one scale and the negatives on the other scale. We do, however, expect the positives side of the scale to crash to the floor. That's the kind of person we're going to hire.

Computer Literacy
Corporate America **demands** a high degree of computer literacy from all development candidates. Quite simply, because

our world is becoming so technologically dependent, the industry **leaders** of the future must be able to function in a complex, rapidly changing environment. The boom in computer use and technology has touched all of business. You will be handicapped if you are learning **both** your job **and** new technology when you start. Today, I can show 38% more positions to applicants with strong computer literacy than to those without it. I don't doubt this percentage will continue to grow.

Due to the changing nature of technology, "literacy" no longer means knowing how to tear apart a mainframe computer. People in industry use personal computers (PCs) that are networked with a mainframe they never see. Therefore, our guidelines focus on ways to improve your literacy through PCs.

Learn On The Most Available PC At Work
The quickest way to learn is to sit down in front of a PC and practice. You can do so with PCs at work. The Army, Navy, and Air Force all use IBM compatible computers, mostly Zenith 248s. Because industry is predominantly IBM or IBM compatible, you can practice now with hardware and software that you will be using in industry.

Specifically:

• Become familiar with Disk Operating System (DOS).

• Learn any software that falls into one of the three main categories of business software: word processing, database, and spreadsheet. Pay special attention to the following brand names, as they are all industry mainstays: DBase IV, WordPerfect, WordStar, Lotus 1-2-3, and Excel.

- To accomplish this, ask the normal operator to help you. Also, refer to the manuals or any tutorials that may be written for beginners.

Take Courses At A Local College
While hands-on practice is invaluable, you will also benefit from refreshing your memory about basic computer theory, languages, and programming.

We recommend some combination of the following sources: Beginning Computers, PC Skills, and Programming (Basic, Cobol, or Pascal). It is difficult to be more specific because each case is unique, and course offerings vary significantly from base to base.

Buy A Personal Computer
We strongly recommend it, and it will be money well spent. Follow these suggestions:

- Carefully determine where you want to buy. You can't go wrong with one of the national chains if your base location puts you close to one of their outlets. If not, there are many excellent smaller dealers. You should really probe into their concept of service. Ask to speak to previous customers. Avoid stores that appear unprofessional — they probably are.

- Buy an IBM or an IBM **compatible. Avoid clones**, i.e., unknown brands or locally assembled PCs. Compatibles are reliable, clones are not. Consider Compaq, HP, Tandy, Dell, Gateway or Zenith.

- The following hardware is strongly recommended, and is worth the price, though at the time the cost may seem high: 2-4MB RAM, 40-80MB hard drive, and a letter quality printer.

* The following software is also suggested: WordPerfect or Microsoft Word for word processing; Excel or Lotus 1-2-3 for spreadsheet; and DBase IV or Paradox for database. Some of the most important money you spend will be on the right software. Include its price in your budgeting.

Finally, remember **you** must improve your literacy. No one can do it for you. Do not rely on what you learned four to five years ago in school. It is outdated. If you are not able to leave the military for several years, make sure a "quality" recruiting firm is keeping you updated on changing technology.

Answering Machines

We require all of our applicants to have answering machines. Today, more than ever before, we have to be extremely concerned about time. We are being asked to do more and more work — you, I, and everyone else — in minimum time. To attempt to call into a military base and leave a message is very difficult. Many times, I leave a message, and if I ask the individual to read it back, he or she says, "I'm sorry. I didn't have a pencil." One recruiter said, "When I call applicants at their homes and there is no answering machine, I will not call back again. What applicants are telling me is that they really don't care about my time. They are wrong. I'm not willing to use my time or my associate's time when there are other applicants with whom we can communicate. An applicant today who doesn't have an answering machine probably doesn't believe in computers either." I encourage you, as you are preparing for your job search, to have an answering machine that has remote capability. If you are traveling on follow-up interviews, you can call in and receive your messages. Once your search is completed, if you wish, you can dispose of the answering machine. You can do so, even though I doubt you will. I believe you will find it a great convenience.

During a career search, record a message on your answering machine that is professional. Come to the point so recruiters or their associates can leave a message and go on about their business. It is not appropriate to use flamboyant messages that demonstrate your talents as a comedian or your love of music. While amusing in a social setting, these messages waste a recruiter's valuable time and do not present the business image you need to project. Also, consider setting your answering machine so that it picks up calls after the first ring. There's no need to waste the caller's time when you're not there to answer.

Should You Use A Recruiting Firm?
Obviously, anyone reading this will feel this is a biased, opinionated statement. To a degree, it is. Nevertheless, the answer is "yes." Without fail, the first thing you should do is become associated with a **quality** recruiting firm. Most companies prefer to go through recruiting firms. If their normal ratio is to interview 200 people to hire one, a company is very reluctant to turn down 199 people who are going to be out on the street potentially buying their product. When rejected applicants reach up on the shelf to buy the product, they may buy a competitor's product just because the other company turned them down.

It's much less expensive to have a recruiting firm say "no" to the majority of applicants. This is why quality recruiting firms are judged based on the factor of 10 interviews. When a company comes to that recruiting firm and interviews 10 people, how many on the average do they say "yes" to? Of every 10 they pursue, how many receive offers? For every 10 who are offered jobs, how many accept? And, for every 10 that accept, how many are successful and promotable? So, recruiting firms are judged very carefully by corporate clients. It will be important for you (in making your decision) to determine which recruiting company to work with. Use a recruiting firm which has developed outstanding relationships with its client companies.

Many of you come to us suggesting that you are represented by two or three recruiting firms. We understand your reasoning. It's just that the more outstanding recruiting firms (ones that do all the work to get an applicant ready) are out a tremendous expense. Obviously, the outstanding recruiting firm is not willing to develop an applicant so the individual can interview on his/her own or through another recruiting firm. If you're going to choose the best recruiting firm in the country, then you need to isolate your loyalty to that company until they have had the chance to show you to client companies. I know of no recruiting firm in America that asks for 100% exclusivity. If they do, walk away from them. However, for a **quality** recruiting firm to ask for exclusivity **until** they have shown you to their clients is simply good business.

Can you do a search on your own? Yes, absolutely. Usually, it is much more costly, but it can be done and done successfully. Handing your resume to one who works for a company and who in turn can hand it to a hiring manager is the best and smartest way to do it. Don't pour resumes through the front door of a company. Thousands are coming to some companies on a weekly basis. So, putting a resume into that mass and hoping a company will call you is going against all odds. Having a friend, acquaintance, or parent hand your resume to a hiring manager of their company can ensure better success than the mail-in route.

Some officers will not earn the right to be represented by a recruiting firm. That's not a harsh statement — it's an honest statement. Every recruiting firm that supports an applicant must ask themselves, "Does my client company need to pay me a fee to find this person?" Unfortunately, many times that answer is a "no." Yet, we know that individual can get hired by a company and be successful. We are not suggesting that the person is not a quality person, but client companies put restrictions on what we can show them.

At our recruiting firm, we have said over the years, "We know we have the knowledge and capability to help a military officer make a successful transition." Candidly speaking, we want to get reimbursed for that effort and knowledge. It's just good business.

Present a quality file to your recruiting firm. Applicants sometimes make statements which cause me to rule them out. They say, "Well, I wouldn't say that to a company." Let me emphasize, "You have just said it to a company." You must remember that a recruiting firm is retained by the corporation. We can't ask you not to make a statement. We can't be unprofessional and suggest you cover up what you said, or say, "Don't dare say that in front of the company; they won't hire you." Applicants have told me they're not sure whether they want to go into the profit-oriented world or into civil service. Can you imagine a company saying, "Roger, we want to pay you $10,000 to find us an individual who's not certain whether they want to operate in the profit-oriented or the nonprofit world." These are diametrically opposed operating philosophies. We're looking for a person who has a **burning desire** to get into the profit-oriented world, be a capitalist, and rise to the top. We must **see** that desire.

Some applicants say, "Several years down the road, I want to own my own business." I have to rule that applicant out. You wouldn't want someone to walk into your place of business to say, "I want you to train me, develop me, and pay me a high salary. Then, I can save money, go across the street, open my own business, and go into competition with you."

I'm not asking you to be dishonest. I am asking you to evaluate what you want to do with your life. If it is to open your own business, I respect that. After all, I own my own business. But don't use somebody else to do it. Just go open your business and be successful. If you want a career in Corporate America, then come committed. Use all of the development my companies will offer. Go to the top. Be a leader within that company. I grant you things can change in the future. But, to start a developmental career with a company knowing you're going to leave them in the near future is purely unprofessional and dishonest.

Give the recruiting firm everything they need to professionally represent you. Type your application. As you have children or your age changes, update your application. Document anything sent to your recruiting firm, and keep a copy yourself. Watch your spelling and sentence structure. Never refer to your resume on your applications. I interview more than 20 people a day. I don't have time to review over 20 different resume formats to find the information you're referencing. Don't be lazy in filling out the application. Show us you believe the application is very important. You want to be represented as the professional person we know you are. Keep the material in your file current as you get new officer evaluations. Don't wait until the last minute to get your college transcripts. Get everything ahead of time.

SLOPPY APPLICATIONS = DECLINE

Many applications cause us to immediately decline. I say to myself, "I don't even want to take the time to type a rejection letter, put a stamp on it, and mail it." This file doesn't warrant taking our time, but, professionally, we do it anyway. As sloppy applications come in, we say to ourselves, "Obviously, this wasn't very important to the applicant because it is so sloppy." These applications could misrepresent you — on the other hand, they may not!

You want to work with a quality recruiting firm. Check out the firm. Ask for applicants they have successfully placed. Ask them about their success rate. How many applicants do they bring to a conference? What percentage of those applicants were successful? You have every right to ask these questions. It's important for you to get a recruiting firm that works for you. Unfortunately, some recruiting firms throughout the United States only send your resume to different companies and hope the companies respond. It is interesting that when they send your resume, they, in effect, attach a bill to it — maybe $2,500 to $3,500, or more. So, unless a recruiting firm is doing a lot for the company — screening you thoroughly by looking at everything you are being evaluated on in the three periods of your life — is that recruiting firm really doing anything for its client company? The great companies in Corporate America are very smart. They put their money where they get the best value.

I've heard applicants say, "I've already been accepted by another recruiting firm." I say, "When were you interviewed?" They answer, "I haven't been interviewed. I was accepted by phone." What would Procter & Gamble, Mobil Oil, Johnson & Johnson, or Michelin say if a recruiting firm calls them to say, "We want you to interview an applicant we haven't seen." Can you imagine that? If a recruiting firm isn't willing to commit the time and expense to come to your base/post and interview you and work with you over a period of time, do you really need them?

As I talk to so many of you, you tell me, "A recruiting firm doesn't want to talk to me unless I'm within three to six months of getting out of the military." Do you realize what that recruiting firm is saying? They're saying they don't want to work with you over a period of time. They don't want to have to educate you. They don't want to look into your background and tell you what you need to do to be better prepared. They don't want to help you develop as an interviewee.

They're saying, "No, we just want to show you to a company, cross our fingers that you get placed, and earn our fee." Make sure the recruiting firm is willing to do the kind of work it will take to develop you over a period of time. You don't need a recruiting firm that looks at you with a dollar figure in mind. Unfortunately, too many recruiting firms in America do just that. When you know major companies are paying top dollar to recruiting firms to select, interview, and bring quality people to them, you have every right to demand certain standards.

The Crucial First Impression

"PCS was second to none in giving me guidance and detailed explanations on what a career in Corporate America is all about. I continue to use the advice and guidance that Roger shares in his book. Preparation and determination are the keys to professional success and, for me, the first step toward early preparation was reading PCS. It is a must for those who want to succeed in a very competitive environment."

— Jorge Perez
Production Manager
SAMCO Scientific
Division of Corning, Inc.

CHAPTER 2

The Crucial First Impression

What is the **first impression** you make to a prospective employer? In the hundreds of speeches I've given around the world, I've often asked my audiences this question. And, in the many years I've been in this business, I have never heard the answer I believe is the correct one.

People say it's the appearance you make as you step into the recruiter's office: your suit, your dress, your grooming — the sparkle in your eyes, your voice inflection, your walk, your handshake. I emphatically believe all these factors make up the **second** impression.

The first impression is your **resume** or **application.** In 99% of these cases, the resume is seen even before an application.

POOR RESUMES/POOR APPLICATIONS = DECLINE

Recruiters, believe it or not, are human beings. As they evaluate your resume, they form an impression. It can be one of tremendous interest — or of no interest at all. Sadly, many times when I look at a resume, it instantly turns me off. Let's focus on what a resume should do for you.

RESUMES: THE VITAL INFORMATION

Availability Date
First and foremost, a resume should tell a recruiter your date of availability. A position is open. The date you are available should coincide with that position being open or when the position **will** be open. You may be the best applicant going — but, if your availability doesn't coincide with the appropriate time for the company, then you're of no value to that company.

Level Of Education
Second, show your level of education. It's important because, often, jobs call for a specific educational background. If your education isn't right, then the corporation will have to walk away from you. If the information on your resume is incomplete, they'll also walk away.

Accomplishments
When you give an example of a significant accomplishment, remember that Corporate America says no accomplishment can be considered significant without a high factor of **difficulty.** Your ability to communicate your accomplishments both in your resume and verbally is most important. If you cannot describe past accomplishments, you will have a very difficult time having a successful interview.

The **difficulty** must come from the objective, not from the element of time. In the military, you were probably given tasks that were difficult because they were dropped on you at the last minute. You had to do them fast. But, in corporate business, it will be the **difficulty of the objective.**

Success is measured by the accomplishment of an objective. Failure is nonaccomplishment of that objective. We can succeed to different degrees. How do you measure the quality of success? You judge it by the factor of **difficulty**. The greater the **difficulty** of the objective, the greater the quality of success.

Let's say two men are commanders of identical military units and situations. At the end of a given time period, their supervisor says he judges them as commanders who are equally good. Both accomplished their missions. But, one commander protests, "No way. While it's true we produced the same performance with identical units, I did it **without** an executive officer for 6 out of 12 months, and with 7% **less** troop strength." Thus, the quality of this commander's success is greater because of the additional **difficulty** factor.

Recently, for example, an applicant asked me my opinion of his resume. "Are you sure you want me to comment?" I asked. He said, "yes" his curiosity aroused. I said, "I'm amazed you would build a resume that suggests you've been a failure."

Why, in fact, was there actually strong proof of failure in his resume? After all, his resume told what his responsibilities were—job title, dates of that position, and the duties assigned to him. He was a company commander, had 120 troops under him, and was responsible for their combat readiness, health and welfare. There were about 8 to 10 lines of this, and then he went on to his previous position. He put down his entire military career.

But, he failed to remember that with any **responsibility**, you can **fail** as well as succeed. You can **fail** to certain degrees. You can **succeed** to certain degrees. What we want to know on your resume, more than anything, is this: When you were given a responsibility, **what did you do with it?** What were your **accomplishments?**

This applicant failed to tell us he had any accomplishments. A recruiter could only assume he had no successes with his responsibilities. Therefore, he was leaving the military for the wrong reasons. No one would have responded to his resume. It was interesting that this applicant proceeded to **prove** that he had been a failure in the military. What he did was this: at the top of his resume under education, he wrote that he had a 3.74 GPA — proving he had been a failure. Do you see it? Don't miss the point that, in fact, what he did was this: he said to the corporate recruiter rating his resume, "I feel it is important that you know how well I did." In other words, he quantified his success academically, showing the importance of quantification. Then, he got into his military experience and didn't put **any** quantification of success. He had already stated he knew the importance of quantification when he stated his GPA, but then didn't do it later. He gave us **proof** that, in fact, he had failed. If he had left the GPA off, we could have simply assumed that he didn't know the importance of quantifying his success, but we still wouldn't have hired him.

Stating Your Objective
Caution: Applicants who are working with a recruiting firm should follow the firm's specific guidelines on objectives. Their system may be designed for better flexibility while interviewing with several companies at one time.

However, if you are mailing your resume, you must have an **objective** on it. Don't be vague or general in your objective. "Position in management, building upon an ability to balance multiple projects while still attaining overall goals by virtue of detailed planning and thoughtful delegation of responsibility." This tells most recruiters that you don't know exactly what you want to do. Furthermore, you have used the words "position in management." Most of the top companies in

Corporate America develop management from within. Consequently, you have just eliminated yourself from many of the top companies in Corporate America. Be careful of the word "management" when, in fact, you mean "supervision."

Frequently, the military officer comes to me and other corporate recruiters and makes the statement that he or she wants to start in one of the following:
• A mid-level management position.
• A lower mid-level management position.
• An upper mid-level management position.
• An entry-level management position.

In the many years I have been recruiting military officers, I have never placed anyone in a management role. My companies simply do not hire management from outside. Imagine yourself working for a company for a four- or five-year period of time, you find a management spot opening up above you, and then the company goes outside to hire someone into that position. You would be very unhappy. You would be demoralized. That company would have a morale problem on its hands.

Frequently, in the military, you misuse the word "management," and confuse it with the word "supervision." Here's how we succinctly articulate the difference between management and supervision. In the military, you're not a manager until you reach the level of colonel or above, because managers set big-picture objectives. Supervisors motivate subordinates to carry out the objectives that management establishes. Therefore, we would even suggest that a company commander would be a supervisor carrying out the objectives that battalion or upper-level management, colonel or above, establishes for them — not that one is good or one is bad — it just clarifies where you are in the company. So, if officers would indicate the word "supervisor," they are looking for a supervisory position instead of a management position, they would find that their resumes would be read and the odds for pursuit would increase.

Give an objective that is **directed**, such as "sales leading to management," "staff engineering," "management information systems," "line operations," "manufacturing," "operations," etc. Be specific. Tell a recruiter you are a person who knows what you want to do. Demonstrate that you have done a thorough analysis, studied Corporate America, and have a good feeling for where you will fit best. Leaving the military as an officer, you are behind your age group who went straight from college to business. Therefore, in order to catch up, you must have conviction plus a definite career objective.

It is better to build two, three or even four different resumes, based on different objectives, than to have one resume with an objective that attempts to cover everything.

Supporting The Primary Objective
One of the most critical points in a resume is that your accomplishments **must support the primary objective** of the position you held.

Let's consider a commander with 120 troops. What do we want to know more than anything else? We want to know that the troops are ready for combat. That's most important. Once a company commander told me his best accomplishment was that his mess hall was voted best mess of the quarter, three quarters in a row. But, the mess hall is a **collateral** mission, not a **primary** one.

If you expect to be a successful supervisor in Corporate America, then you should highlight (in your accomplishments) what you did with your supervisory experience. Tell about your successes in motivating subordinates. I have many applicants who write in their resumes or verbalize to me all of the significant accomplishments they had with those they supervised. You must understand that some supervisors (to achieve an accomplishment) burn up their people. They mishandle their people. They use negative motivation and, therefore, have a heavy turnover. The focus must be on the people themselves. The accomplishment of the objective in a professional manner is important. We are interested in hiring development managers who understand that keeping turnover low and morale high is extremely important. Again, you must be careful. You cannot **tell** us you do this. You must **show** us, quantifiably, what you have done for your people.

If your primary job objective is an engineering position, then show the recruiter your accomplishments (in the military or wherever) in engineering. Always remember, your accomplishments must draw as close a parallel as possible to the position for which you are interviewing. It's fine to list collateral successes — but they should be secondary on a resume.

Quantifying Your Successes
As you build your resume, the **extent** of your success, the **quantification** of it, is the key factor. In order to know this quantification was successful, we have to know what the **goal** was. For example, if you reached a vehicle readiness factor of 95%, let us know this was, say, 3% above objective, or whatever the case may be. Sadly, too many officers (as they interview with me) prove by their rhetoric that they probably should stay in the world of nonprofit. They are constantly wanting to tell me how they developed a new training program. But, they never bothered to tell me what the training program actually accomplished. They say they designed a new

transportation system, never bothering to tell me how that new system impaced the bottom line. They may tell me they designed a new software program, but again they put their emphasis on the fact that they designed it — not what it accomplished. So, be very careful that you learn the language of industry. Everything we do in industry must impact the bottom line of the company — saving man hours, increasing profitability, lowering cost, etc.

Often, an officer tells me, "I improved the morale of my unit." You need to show how it was done. What percent increase did you have in reenlistment? What percent decrease did you have in troops going AWOL? What decrease did you have in Article 15s? You must give **proof and evidence** of what you say. Rhetoric alone won't suffice.

The preceding applicant also told me, "But, Roger, I spent $75 to get that resume built by a resume service." I'm sorry if I step on toes here. Too many times resume services are more interested in making a resume look pretty — focusing on how it's typed and the kind of paper used. I maintain that if these resume services charged you according to the **success** the resume produces, they might get more serious about how they pull it all together.

Your resume must represent bottom-line qualities and **attract** a company to you.

Common Misconceptions
Many officers feel their resumes should be on the best bond paper. I agree. But, the **content** is what's important. I've had recruiters tell me, "I don't care if they write it on paper grocery bags, as long as the content is right, and we can get the information we need."

I actually recommend two different resume formats. If you're leaving the military interviewing for a non-development position, it might be better to exclude extracurricular activities in high school and college. However, the majority of you will want to come to Corporate America and get into a development position. About the only difference between the two resume formats we give you is that one shows extracurricular activities in high school and college; the other does not. If you're interviewing for a development position and hoping to be a top manager, keep in mind that most companies find top managers have successful traits in common, even in high school. As a development candidate, it's important, therefore, to show the extracurricular activities you had in high school and college. If you're entering business as a computer expert, you may not have to list these. Over the years I've discovered these activities **are** very important — if you want a top leadership role with a major company.

The resume format I give you is based on the years I've spent recruiting officers and working daily with companies. I asked these firms the following question: What do you want to see in a resume to obtain the information you need? I want to note here that I have been in a business where I am paid only for bottom-line performance, not for my opinion. This fact lends a lot of credibility to this resume format.

This format reflects the feelings of some of the top corporate recruiters in America. They told me exactly what they needed to know — and what format to use.

Most resumes should be held to one page. But, don't be afraid to go beyond that if the information is relevant and presented in an articulate, succinct manner.

Resume Format Suggestions

The resume format I suggest is one that has been very success-ful for the candidates I have recruited. I think you will find this format to be an excellent one. Turn to the resume formats in Appendix E. Note that there are resumes for both develop-ment and non-development candidates. Use these resumes and the following instructions to determine how to format your resume. Be careful and thorough and type your resume using the samples and the following instructions as a guide.

- Use 1/2 inch margins for each side. (Do not make them wider. Applicants often set margins at 1/2 inch, indent a bit further and add additional space between bullets and text, and the resulting space between text and paper edge is 1 inch to 1 1/2 inches.)

- Begin 1.7 inches from the top of the page. (If you are working with a recruiting firm, you may need to start lower to account for the firm's letterhead.)

- Single space your resume.

- Do not add more than one line between sections of the resume.

- Leave at least 1/2 inch at the bottom of the page.

- **Personal Information:** At the top left of your resume, type your name, address, city, state, nine-digit zip code, and your home phone number (including your area code).

- **Availability Date:** Approximately 4 1/2 inches from the left margin, type your availability date, written as month, day, and year. [Your availability date should be determined by subtracting your total amount of terminal leave (which you continue to accrue while on terminal leave) from your ETS, or last date of official service. **Be sure to use the earliest possible date.**]

- **Physical Information:** Below your availability date, add your age, height, and weight. Below this, add your marital status ("Single" or "Married").

- **Education Information:** This section should include all your undergraduate and graduate degrees and/or additional coursework. Type your undergraduate degree(s) on the left below your personal information and your graduate degree(s) and coursework below the availability date. [Your resume entries should match your college transcript entries for the degree(s) you were awarded. Many graduates have shortened their degree titles for convenience. **Refer to your transcripts to be sure of your degree title.** If you took a lot of courses in finance, that doesn't mean you had a minor in finance. If your transcript doesn't show it, don't put it on your resume. Some companies request transcripts, and if there is a discrepancy, it will be a significant strike against you.]

- **Activities:** Many of the junior officers with whom we work have distinguished themselves not only academically, but also in extracurricular endeavors. List both high school and college activities on the resume.

For both high school and college, list the following: all scholastic honors and scholarships (except ROTC scholarships); honorary societies; student body government; class organizations; clubs; publications; assistantships; community, civic, or church memberships; and offices to which you were nominated or elected.

For any society, student body, class government, organization, or club in which you held an office or had a unique organization-specific accomplishment, include that office or accomplishment in parentheses following the entry — for example, "Debate Club (President, First Place State Forensic Tournament)."

For any athletic activity, annotate with "varsity," "junior varsity," "freshman," "club," or "intramural status" (mention only the highest level achieved). If you received awards or honors, enter them parenthetically as above—for example, "Varsity Football (Co-Captain, All-Conference, State Champions)."

- If you have worked full-time or part-time in either high school or college, enter the following statement in the section(s) in which it applies: "Worked part- (or full-) time, ___ hours per week, during ___ (school and/or summers)." Fill in the appropriate hours you worked. (If you did not work, do not include the statement. Academy graduates should not include this statement in their college activities section.)

Immediately below the last line of your college activities section (do not skip a line) enter educational financing information. Type "**Note**:" followed by an explanation of how you paid for your undergraduate **and** graduate degrees. [Determine how you financed your degrees — through full- or part-time work (yours), your parents, scholarships (lump grants and other funding that were not repayable with scholarships), or loans. Use percentages and **ensure all funding types added together equal 100%**. Then, enter the percentages on the resume, starting with the largest percentage first — for example, "60% of undergraduate education financed by full-time work, 40% by loan."]

Experience: Below your educational financing entry, enter your **military** experience. Provide the dates of your active duty service, your military rank, your specialty, and your branch.

Next, enter your military work history. This is the most important part of your resume. Describe your duties and accomplishments for each position you held starting with the most recent job. For each position, enter four key elements:

1) *Date:* Enter dates of service by month and year.

2) *Job Title:* **For the vast majority of jobs, enter the technically correct title.** [Refer to your evaluations. Some job titles are not helpful to a recruiter, and you can't afford to spend your interview explaining what a title means. Therefore, you need to find a balance between what is technically correct (on your officer evaluations) and what is descriptive. However, **do not attempt to civilianize this or any other part of your resume.**]

3) *Responsibilities:* Enter three to five lines of information about your specific responsibilities for each job you list. (Refer to your officer evaluations. Be sure to include your supervisory responsibilities — number and type of personnel supervised. Be as specific as possible. The terms "mechanic," "electrician," "machinist," and "clerk" are more effective than "soldier." Also, discuss the amount and type of equipment for which you were responsible.)

4) *Accomplishments:* Enter the accomplishments you have achieved for each job you list. Each accomplishment should stand on its own, in a "bullet" format. (Describe

your accomplishments with action verbs. **Quantify your accomplishments**, or in other words, make your accomplishments measurable. For example, "Greatly reduced paperwork" is a vague achievement; many recruiters would question what "greatly" means.)

The following are some sample bullets:

- Achieved 95% operational readiness rating, 5% over objective.

- Recognized for having Best Platoon in battalion.

- Achieved 2 successive above average grades on Operational Reactor Safeguard Examinations.

- Maintained project status on time despite 55% cut in budget funding.

- Reduced payroll discrepancies from 23% to 5% in 3 months.

- Awarded division's "MacArthur Leadership Award."

- **Civilian Experience:** Below your military experience, enter any jobs you have held as a civilian that may enhance your marketability. Type **"CIVILIAN EMPLOYMENT"** in all caps and bold. One space below that, begin your civilian experience as you did above for the military. Enter the dates, your title, and where you worked. Then, enter a description of your duties. (Do not detail your accomplishments; there will be no room for bullets in civilian experience. Areas you should include are the following: engineering, co-ops, lab assistantships, running your own business, computer work, or any job that relates to your experience. Do **not** include jobs in fast food, grounds maintenance, dorm resident assistantship, basic office administration, and other less important areas. While we do not want to diminish the importance of these types of jobs, in terms of marketability, they are less relevant than your military career.)

The Cover Letter

When you **mail** your resume, it is crucial to send a cover letter. The letter must be written specifically to that company. Do not send generic cover letters. You're telling the company all they need to know to decline you. Don't be lazy. **The resume must be able to stand on its own.**

Often, your cover letter will be removed from the resume when the resume is forwarded to hiring managers. The managers will be unaware of any cover letter. If you've put important information in this letter, it's likely to stay with the personnel director to whom you addressed it.

Make powerful statements in the letter. What can you offer that is relevant to that particular company? What are your abilities and career accomplishments? Why do you have a real interest in this corporation? Remember, keep the letter company-specific.

I consider your resume to be one of the most critical aspects of your job search. It's the primary factor, so do it first. You must have **documentation** on paper, listing who you are and what you're all about, along with your past performance. I find that too many applicants spend very little time on their resumes. What they produce simply isn't enough.

When you walk through the door for an interview, you want to know that you're in front of a recruiter who — through reading your resume — already has a very positive attitude about you — a positive first impression.

APPLICATIONS

Your application to a company (the actual application form) is a document that will represent you for the balance of your career if you go to work for that company. **Think about that.** It must be completed in a manner that you would always want in your permanent records.

This form may be the first impression a company representative has of you. Don't underestimate its importance. Think carefully as you complete the basic form.

Follow these basic rules:

1) **Carefully** follow the specific instructions, such as "Print" or "List last position first."

2) Type the application whenever possible, unless you are specifically instructed to do otherwise. If printing, be neat. Always use dark ink, preferably black. There should be no mark-outs. You may use a small amount of correcting fluid, but not correction tape.

3) Check for correct **spelling**, correct **grammar**, and correct **punctuation**. Use a dictionary.

4) Don't leave blanks. If a question doesn't apply to you, put a short dash in the space, write "None," or write "N/A" (Not Applicable). **Complete the entire form**; don't skip questions.

5) Fill in the entire space provided for an answer. If, for example, there are three lines to list school activities, fill in all three lines.

6) **Never put "See Resume."** The company representatives know they can look at your resume. Your application must be able to stand alone and apart from your resume. It must clearly represent your entire experience and qualifications. Put all the information **where the company wants it:** on their application.

7) Avoid attaching an addendum or additional sheet. Although a form may state, "Feel free to attach supplemental information," the attached sheet can become detached — and then vital information will be lost. If there are four spaces provided for work history, and you had six jobs in the military, use two of the spaces for two jobs each. **Your entire military background should be divided so that all your positions are included in the spaces provided.** **Do not** use just **one** space to indicate several years of military job experience, then the remaining three spaces for less notable work.

8) If asked to state "Reason for seeking change" or "Reason for leaving" a past or a present position, **do** give an answer. In the military, it may be due to promotion, change of duty, normal rotation, etc. But, your reason for leaving your **current** military position should be carefully worded. Don't say, "Completed military obligation." That shows no interest or conviction to make industry your career. A **positive**, goal-oriented answer would be, "Desire to pursue a career in major industry." **Use your own words.**

You'll find three **caution areas** that are especially sensitive subjects on many applications. Here's how to deal with them.

- **Salary.** Answer "Open or negotiable." Please note this is **not** the way you would handle this question in an interview itself. **But**, an application cannot elaborate. It can't modify. You don't dare allow the application to get you ruled out because you put a dollar figure that doesn't allow latitude. This allows you to discuss the entire subject of compensation in person, with the company representative. It indicates salary is just one of many items you'll consider when making a career decision.

* **Location.** Always state "Open" on the application. **Again, this is completely different from what you would do in the interview itself.** If the word "open" is used in an interview, it will frequently disqualify you. If this question has two parts — "Do you have a preference?" and "Do you have any restrictions?" — answer the first by stating a broad geographical preference, such as "the Northeast," "the southern United States," "east of the Mississippi River," etc. Answer the second question, "None." If you know the location of the job for which you're interviewing, you can tailor your answer to that area. For example, you can state a preference of "east of the Mississippi" with "no" restrictions. National companies hire people they can promote without severe geographical restrictions.

* **Position Desired/Objective.** Always **state precisely** the position title/objective. State only **one** objective per application, even if the application provides space for more than one position title.

The application is tangible, permanent evidence of your ability to answer specific questions and organize your ideas accurately and concisely.

CHAPTER 3

Preparing For The Interview

"The most powerful tool on today's market to help you attain career search success is <u>PCS to Corporate America</u>. Roger Cameron will guide you through every step to ensure that you are headed in the right direction throughout the military and into your career. Don't waste a single minute of your time not knowing the precise direction you should be taking. Read this book now and you will be on your way to attaining your goals. Roger helped me attain mine, and I know he can help you with this book!"

> — Margaret Vallejo
> QualityAssurance Facilitator
> Ethicon Endo-Surgery,
> Division of Johnson & Johnson

CHAPTER 3

Preparing For The Interview

What makes successful interviewing? That's simple — **preparation.** Preparation includes the following:

- A thorough understanding of yourself
- An analysis of what has made you successful
- The ability to communicate those successes in a fluid, persuasive manner

Sounds easy, doesn't it? But, it isn't. Many applicants feel they have the ability to take any subject matter and speak about it — "off the cuff" in an articulate, concise, convincing manner. Unfortunately, few actually can. As a matter of fact, I'm not sure I've ever met anyone during my recruiting career — over 2,000 applicants a year — who got a job without interview preparation. Corporate recruiters are adamant that applicants prepare well for interviewing. As I mentioned in the foreword, companies reason that if applicants do not work hard to prepare for something as valuable as their own career, why should any company dare to believe they're going to work hard to accomplish an objective for their employer? I think this reasoning is very accurate.

You must dedicate time to prepare. Set aside a specific period of time — an hour a day, two hours a day, five hours a week, one-half day a week, Saturday morning, Sunday afternoon — well in advance of interviews with corporate recruiters. You must find the time to read books, to do work assignments, and to prepare for the key questions you know will be asked of you.

I often use this example: If you know you are going to have an annual inspection on Monday morning, you wouldn't begin preparing for it Friday evening. If you did, you certainly know what the outcome would be. You wouldn't prepare on Friday evening for deployment to the National Training Center for a 30-day period of time, knowing that you're leaving on Monday morning. You wouldn't head for REFORGER in January and start working on it the weekend before. Preparation is mandatory for quality results. Can you imagine leaving for a six-month deployment without preparation?

FORTUNE 500 companies can go to the top school campuses in America and put GPA limitations at 3.5. They won't interview anyone below it and can have the best of the best. These are the same companies who will interview you. You have to be good. There's nothing automatic. The fact that you were good in high school, college, and the military does not automatically guarantee you a career in Corporate America. There's just that little thing called an interview that stands between you and success. Think about it for a moment. You're over 27 years old and in an interview. Somebody is asking you to communicate your life in a 30- to 45-minute period of time. It sounds absurd when you think about it, but that is what will happen. So, if you don't know what part of your experience a company is interested in, how can you expect to be successful? Too many applicants feel being successful is buying a great suit or shoes, but that's only a minor part of it.

I've talked to many officers who interviewed with Corporate America without adequate preparation and never received offers. Consequently, without really wanting to, they stayed in the military. I honestly believe that, in many cases, they were rejected by Corporate America not because of their credentials, but because of their inability to **communicate** those credentials. It would be nice if you could get hired on the basis of a resume or an application. But, it's just not possible. I've never known one of my client companies to hire an applicant sight unseen. So, please, dedicate yourself early in this book to preparing for a very difficult venture — interviewing.

Objective/Subjective Assets

It is important for you to understand objective and subjective assets as you prepare for interviewing. Highlight or flag this section so that when you begin your actual preparation, you will start with this topic.

When I ask applicants during the interview process what objective assets they will bring to an employer on the first day, they frequently have no answer. Recruiters will ask this question in one form or another. It's important for you to understand the concepts in order to reply intelligently. Comprehension is critical to effectively market yourself.

The cornerstone of self-evaluation is an understanding of your objective and subjective assets. **An objective asset is one that establishes a point of fact. It is subject to verification.** On the other hand, **a subjective asset is a conditional value, one that is a matter of opinion. It is not subject to independent verification.**

In the interviewing context, you bring a company both subjective and objective assets. Certain objective assets such as academic degrees or leadership experience are non-debatable. The objective asset requirement may also change from interview to interview, depending on the needs of the interviewing company.

Your subjective assets are characteristics, competencies, or behavioral traits such as poise, self-confidence, organizational skills, or attitude. The interviewing company will evaluate these as a matter of opinion or interpretation based on your actions and communication skills in the interview itself.

Objective Asset = Objective Value

(When the asset is required by the company)

For an objective asset to become an objective **value**, it must be **required** by the employer.

To more fully understand objective value, let's say Company XYZ calls me to recruit engineers with leadership experience. In essence, Company XYZ is stating that, "objectively speaking," applicants must have an engineering degree and leadership experience to interview with them. These two required assets are an **objective** value to Company XYZ. In addition to these two required assets, Company XYZ states strong computer literacy will be helpful, but not required. If you have an engineering degree and leadership experience, you have the objective assets required to interview with Company XYZ. Now, let's say you are very computer literate, but your skills are not comparable to those of a computer science major. Your computer literacy will be considered objective **value-added**. If you have an MBA, but it is not required, it will be considered additional objective **value-added**. Realize that what is value-added for one company may be required by another.

Let's consider this scenario: Ms. Hildebrand from ABC, Inc. calls to ask me to recruit development candidates for her. My first question is, "What are you looking for?" She says, "Roger, I want business degreed students with GPAs of 3.0 or above—

individuals who have participated in varsity sports or elected leadership roles and who are able to start work by September 15." If you have these objective asets, you now have the qualificiations to interview with ABC, Inc. Ms. Hildebrand then reviews the **subjective assets** her company values. She says, "We're looking for individuals with strong work ethics. I want someone who is willing to work hard to earn their pay. We insist on goal-oriented, 'make-it-happen' types." Ms. Hildebrand explains that goal-oriented means the willingness to establish or accept high goals that are difficult — but, more importantly, the discipline to FIGHT through ADVERSITY to accomplish those goals. In addition, her company wants people who are team players, who are creative, innovative thinkers, who have vision, and who have pleasant personalities. This scenario is just one example. There are numerous variations of objective and subjective values derived from company job descriptions.

To prepare for the interview process, list all of the objective assets you possess that will be of **value** to companies. Stretch your imagination! Over the years, I have been given unique requirements. I once was told by a company that they needed applicants with 3.0 GPAs or higher who had lived in the South and were six feet tall or taller! The last two requirements could be considered unusual — but, requirements nonetheless. Remember that if the asset is **required**, it becomes an objective value to the company. For most positions, your objective assets determine your functional value to Corporate America. Your objective assets actually get you in the door and allow you to interview. Some of your objective assets will be value-added. The more assets you have, the broader your marketability. It is really very simple:

> **More Objective Assets = More Doors of Opportunity**

Exceptions to this rule are sales positions that may require no specific objective value. In other words, the type of academic degree you have is immaterial. It could be any degree. In fact, the recruiter may not even bother with objective value, but will concentrate only on your subjective assets. For some sales positions, a specific degree is important to have — for instance, when the product is very technical. In that case, a corresponding technical degree is required. It would then be necessary for you to have an objective asset (technical degree) before you could interview with the company.

While objective assets will get you in the door, subjective assets will get you hired. Therefore, your preparation for interviews must also include analysis of your subjective assets and, most of all, practice in articulating them. You should be able to describe your subjective assets with examples of accomplishments that illustrate the use of these assets. What do you consider to be your strengths and distinguishing characteristics? Think in terms of what is most important to recruiters. Companies look for certain assets in applicants, such as initiative, creativity, enthusiasm, conceptual and analytical skills, persuasive communication, being a team player, and interpersonal skills. Make sure your subjective assets are valuable to companies.

Next, take your 5 or 6 most important subjective assets and practice illustrating them in your answers to interviewing questions such as, "Tell me about a significant problem and how you solved it." "Tell me about a significant accomplishment and how you accomplished it."

Speak into a tape recorder and ask someone else to listen to the tape to determine how well you illustrated your assets. If the illustration is not clear to them, it will not be clear to the recruiter.

Remember to be yourself in interviews. Maintain your individuality. Your experiences are yours. Your assets, objective and subjective, are yours. You are unique. You have created a "product" which you are selling to a recruiter. The recruiter must see your strengths and be able to determine how well you will fit into their company. You must verbally create a picture that effectively illustrates your ability to join the company and make a significant contribution.

While the foundation of a successful interview is knowing your subjective and objective assets, you cannot get away with simply "laundry listing" those assets to a recruiter.

You must be able to evaluate the recruiter's questions and tailor your answers to fit their specific job needs. You must be able to consistently and persuasively articulate your assets by the examples you give in the interview.

General Store Analogy
An analogy that has proven to be beneficial in "translating" successes in your background into success in the interview is called the "General Store" analogy. This exercise takes you to the next step by defining a method to effectively market your listed assets in the interview much like a store owner markets products in a store.

Think back to the western movies which showed a general merchandise store. The assorted products, such as nails, gloves, tools, buttons, thread, etc., were arranged in various drawers and cubbyholes in a shelving unit. The General Store owner assisted customers with their shopping lists, matching needs to products in the shelves. Each customer had a different request, and the owner was the product expert who knew the best product to fit the need. No one knew the products better and no one had more to gain from the sale.

Customer service was the priority — making certain the customer was satisfied and their needs were fulfilled.

Now, picture your own General Store. The product line consists of your objective and subjective assets. You have actually taken your asset list and stocked the shelves. You have many assets supported by examples and evidence to assure your inventory is very marketable. Your customer, the recruiter, enters your store with needs which you, as the store owner, must fulfill. You must evaluate and select the "best" product that matches or fits the company's requirements. Your selection and evaluation of the "best" product is critical. Just as the store owner reviews and evaluates the customer's needs, so must you evaluate the recruiter's needs. After all, the store owner would not sell a hammer to someone who wanted to paint a fence.

Your examples and evidence, concisely articulated, sell the product, your assets, to the recruiter. Remember: **No one knows the product better and no one has more to gain from the sale**. Just as the General Store owner wants to satisfy the customer's needs and sell their products, you want to "fit" the recruiter's needs and sell your assets!

Your ability to effectively match your assets to the recruiter's needs will be a key factor for success in your interviews. You see, the recruiter knows exactly what they are looking for in terms of a perfect "fit" for their company. You must have the ability to persuasively convince the recruiter that your total product (your objective and subjective assets) is **exactly** what the company needs!

Most applicants try to force the exact same objective and subjective assets on every recruiter. This works no better than the General Store owner trying to sell the exact same merchandise to every customer. Customers all have different and specific needs . . . just like the recruiter. The General Store owner must evaluate and identify each customer's needs in order to make the sale. You, too, must evaluate and identify each recruiter's needs to "fit" and sell your assets. When you understand and apply this concept to your interviewing skills, it has a powerful impact. Don't be **lazy** in implementing this concept!

Developing Self-Insight

Corporate recruiters constantly ask me to be sure to bring them people who have the ability to look in the mirror, see exactly what's there, know who they are, and have the self-confidence to be able to tell a company what they're all about. On his application for a career objective, one officer wrote CEO. Obviously, the minute he put that down as an objective, it was my job to see if there was proof and evidence that he could accomplish his objective.

I went back to his high school information to check how many times he had been number one. He certainly hadn't graduated from high school as number one. He had a 3.1 GPA. I also looked to see how many times he had been elected to leadership roles. There were none. His college GPA was 2.7. He was not president of his class, student body president, or, for that matter, captain of any athletic teams. I said, "Surely I'll find it in the military." I went to his military evaluations expecting, of course, to see only top-block evaluations. Again, there were none. I asked this individual one question. What do you feel are the odds you would be promoted to LCDR below the zone? He laughed at me. He suggested it would be very doubtful. With that, of course, I eliminated him. After all, if you can't be promoted below the zone to LCDR in the Navy where the statistics will actually be greater in your favor, it is unlikely you're going to leave the military and become CEO of IBM, DuPont, Procter & Gamble, Xerox, or Mobil Oil.

When I declined this individual, he said, "Roger, that's not fair. You're suggesting that I shouldn't have high objectives." I looked at the young man and said, "Please don't say that. Don't even suggest it. You must have high goals. You must have goals which make you perspire — goals that make you use every asset of your being to accomplish. But, they must be realistic goals." To become CEO can be a personal goal, but it should never appear on your application. It will do you more harm than good. Remember, there is nothing wrong with ending up in the top 10% of a company's management structure. Play it safe. Have high goals, but be totally objective as to your ability.

Most applicants feel it necessary to say, "I'm a 9 or a 10" in everything they do. Don't get yourself in a job you're not going to be able to handle. I encourage you to be realistic. We have the ability to recruit the very best from college campuses such as Harvard, Wharton, Stanford, University of Chicago, Duke, and other top schools across the country. Remember that we're accustomed to having the very best. You must relate yourself and your skills to those people who are coming out of top schools with top GPAs. We know you have a great ability to perform, but we still want you to realize exactly who you are and what your values are to the military and to Corporate America. Recruiters are looking for applicants who are **realistic** about their abilities regarding promotion opportunities and job performance. **I can't count the number of officers I've seen ruled out because of inflated self-value. Remember this point.**

Covering Your Weaknesses
As I interview military officers, they want to talk about

positives and strengths. Yet, recruiters want to talk about their negatives, and applicants **haven't** prepared themselves to discuss this topic. Great marketing companies in America have taught their sales people how to cover the negatives of a product. They spend as much time learning how to cover the product negatives as they do covering the positives. Positives sell themselves, but negatives will cause you to be ruled out of an interview.

One way to think about weaknesses is to analyze your strengths in relation to others. As you can see in the graph below, there are two strength lines: your normal strength line and your age group strength line. Your normal strength line is higher than the strength line for most people in your age group. There are those in your age group who did not finish high school, did not attend college, and have not had quality successes. The graph illustrates that any characteristic you would describe as "less than a strength" still would not qualify as a "weakness" as it would for most people in your age group. Those characteristics that are described as "less than a strength" are those that do not cause us to fail in the accomplishment of an objective. Unfortunately, recruiters won't ask you for "a less than a strength." They will ask for a weakness (or weaknesses). If you have a **consistent** weakness, do you really think they will hire you?

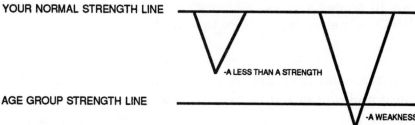

YOUR NORMAL STRENGTH LINE

-A LESS THAN A STRENGTH

AGE GROUP STRENGTH LINE

-A WEAKNESS

Now, how do you answer the question, "What are your weaknesses?" First, be honest. If you truly have a weakness, state it but with qualifiers such as "on **rare** occasions" and "**very** seldom." For example, if you feel you have an occasional problem managing time efficiently, you could say, "On **rare** occasions" or "**very** infrequently." "There have been a **couple** of times I feel I could have better managed my time." You've been candid, but, in reality, have described an occasional "less than a strength" as a weakness. By using the **strong** qualifiers we suggest, you are leaving an important impression — that your weaknesses "rarely" or "seldom" present a challenge to the achievement of your objectives. Again, the key in describing weaknesses ("less than a strength") is to emphasize the fact that you experience them very infrequently.

In addition to using qualifiers to modify a weakness, identify **specifically** what you are doing to overcome the weakness. Using the example of a weakness in time management, you could suggest a definite process you have established to ensure good planning. You might say, "I can specifically remember a couple of situations during my four years in the military that could have been more efficiently managed. Now, each time I find myself in a planning mode, I walk through three specific steps. First, I focus on the objective of the event. Second, I coordinate the event activities to coincide with the time the event must be accomplished, and, third, I put solutions in place for any common problem that could interfere with the timely completion of the event."

Remember that the primary reasons recruiters ask you to discuss your weaknesses are to determine your ability to be honest and candid and to identify what you are **specifically** doing to correct your weaknesses. To communicate that you are always perfect is to be less than honest and will cause a recruiter to determine that you are unqualified for the position.

When you discuss your weaknesses, be careful that you do not preface your remarks by saying, "One of my weaknesses . . . ." Applicants do this frequently. When it occurs, a recruiter is forced to examine the **other** weaknesses that are inferred by this statement. The amount of time in the interview that you have to emphasize your achievements is then limited because the recruiter is focusing on a discussion of your weaknesses.

Most weaknesses are subjective, and most negatives are objective. I encourage you to be honest with yourself. Sit down and list anything which could be perceived as a weakness or negative in your background. Be thorough. Be practical. It is important to confront a negative. Don't brush it off. Don't push it to the side. Don't try to convert a negative to a positive. Most of them won't convert. Take time to examine the negatives and prepare your response. Some negatives might be an irrelevant baccalaureate degree, a low grade point average, quality of the college, more than four years to get a college degree, or being on your fourth career decision at 26 — law school, civil service, military, now Corporate America.

Preparing To Discuss Failure
It is critically important that you go into any interview prepared to discuss a failure. Remember that a failure is simply the non-accomplishment of an objective. It isn't necessarily earth-shattering. It won't necessarily wind up on the front page of *USA Today*.

"Roger, I got caught off guard," an applicant sometimes says to me. "They asked me for a failure. I couldn't come up with one." **Don't let this happen to you.** There can be no excuse for that. There are two key factors about a failure that are important.

1) Companies want to see that you have enough self-confidence to be honest and forthright in describing a failure.

2) They also want to know what you **learned specifically** from the failure and what **broad** application this has for your future.

Companies will determine that if you have never failed, you've probably set your objectives too low. Before hiring, companies want to know how an applicant **reacted** to an adverse situation. A top recruiter once told me, "I want to see someone who has crashed into a brick wall. I want to know how they've reacted — if they've **learned** from the failure. Please don't bring me anyone who hasn't failed." I absolutely agree, so be prepared to discuss a failure. And, don't be talked out of it. Once you've given a failure, accept responsibility for it, even if the failure was due to a subordinate who worked for you. **Never attempt to justify the failure.**

The best example of failure you can give is one for which you were solely responsible. It came from your lack of performance, inefficient time management, lack of organizational planning, prioritizing, or overall ineffective management. Remember, quality people do not justify failure — they learn from it.

When you discuss a failure with a recruiter, explain **why** you failed, how you **reacted,** and what you specifically **learned**. What you learn must have broad applicability in the future. State how the failure encouraged you to improve skills in planning, organizing, communicating, analyzing, and delegating, but be specific. A recruiter wants to know that you can take an adverse situation and analyze how you would improve, with or without a manager to tell you what to do. Recently, an applicant told me that what she learned from a failure was that the next time she purchased specific component parts for her computer department, she would be sure to check with her boss to determine her pricing latitude. While it may have been the policy for her to check with her supervisor, she also could have analyzed her skills more thoroughly. She might have determined that she needed to be more detail-oriented or that she needed to improve her planning skills. The latter analysis is much more broad-based and can have a continuous positive impact on her career.

What Do You Do When Confronted With Failure?

This is a question often used as an eliminator. I encourage you to look hard at this question. It is a question that is similar to being handed a stick of dynamite with a one-inch lit fuse. Be careful of it. Most people fail to note the key word, **"confronted."** Here is the normal response I hear. "Well, the first thing I would do is analyze why I failed." We say, "But you haven't failed." What you've just told the company is, "The first thing I would do is proceed to fail, then I would turn around and analyze it." We don't think that is very smart.

Let's look at this situation for a moment. I tell you, "You're coming to my hotel to interview with me. The road that you normally travel is blocked. Maybe it's being torn up to put in a new sewer system. Maybe a tanker truck turned over on it. What would you do?" You might say, "Well, I can't go down the road, so I'll turn around and go back home." Do you really? I doubt it. I think most of you would determine an alternative route to accomplish your objective. If I pointed that out, most of you would say, "Of course, that's what I would do." Yet, when we ask you what you would do, you talk about the failure.

The best answer I ever received to this question came from an Army captain from Fort Bragg, North Carolina. I'll never forget it. She looked at me and, using hand gestures, said, "I can tell you one thing, Mr. Cameron — I wouldn't fail. If I can't get up the hill one way (she used her left hand to point), then I'll come up the other way (using her right hand to point a different direction)." I don't care what the specific words were, her answer was beautiful. She wasn't going to allow some simple barrier to make her stop.

A good friend of mine who recruits for Procter & Gamble looked at me and said, "Roger, please bring me people who can **make things happen**. I don't want you recommending people to me who, the minute the going gets tough, simply throw up their hands and accept the failure. That is not what we're looking for. We want people who can work through difficult situations, solve problems, and accomplish their objectives."

In a recent trip to the Norfolk area, I asked this question of one of my officers there. The officer looked at me and gave me an answer. I looked at that officer and said, "I'm going to tell you something. In 27 + years of recruiting, that's the worst answer I've ever heard." I have to admit, I sat that individual back a little bit in his chair. I went on to say that I hear that answer far too frequently. The individual said, "The first thing I do when I am confronted with failure is reanalyze the objective." You can't get a more unsuitable answer than that. In other words, he will analyze his objective and lower it. If all we had to do was lower our objective every time we were confronted with failure, nobody would ever fail.

Another frequent response is, "Well, the first thing I do when confronted with failure is let my boss know of a pending failure." My response is always the same. "God forbid you work for Roger Cameron because it's only going to happen one time. I hire people to lay solutions at my feet — **not problems**."

To go through this book and simply learn answers to questions isn't what this book is all about. I expect you to analyze yourself and ask yourself, "Am I really a make-it-happen type of person? When I confront failure, do I do something about it? Does my mind automatically go to an excuse rationalizing why it is all right to fail? Or, do I automatically figure out a different solution to accomplish the objective?" If it isn't the latter, do yourself a favor and stay out of Corporate America. It is an extremely competitive environment. Those people who do not have the ability to find solutions to difficult tasks will fail.

Can you imagine a top *FORTUNE 500* company coming to me and saying, "Roger, we would like to pay you a good fee to travel around the world and find us people who, when confronted with problems, give them back to us." Wouldn't that be absurd? Quite the contrary, companies come to me and say, "Roger, bring me people who can put solutions, not problems, at my feet." I can never comprehend hiring anybody and paying them an outstanding salary to lay problems at my feet. I can do that myself. Don't miss this loaded question. Be careful. The question can be asked many ways using many different words. It won't necessarily be asked as obviously as I've asked it. It's the concept you must understand.

A Word About GPA

Everyone we hire in Corporate America can't have a grade point average of 3.8 or 4.0. That might be nice, but it's unrealistic. Is there anything wrong with a low GPA? Maybe. If you don't have the ability to **convert** the GPA into outstanding performance, then, yes, there's something wrong with it.

I want you to realize we consider a GPA to be an **indicator**. It's really proof of nothing. It's an indication that you're going to be an average performer or below-average performer, depending on the GPA. But the **real** proof of your abilities lies in your evaluations as an officer. We ask this question: Can the GPA be converted to bottom-line performance? Unfortunately, I've seen applicants with high GPAs who were unable to do this, and I have brought in some absolutely outstanding people who held low GPAs. One young man, for example, had a 2.0 GPA, but every one of his OERs was outstanding. He was consistently rated by his superiors as the best they'd supervised. He was able to convert the knowledge he gained from academics to bottom-line military performance. Under no circumstances am I suggesting you be casual about a low GPA. But, I want you to understand, as you enter Corporate America, that education is considered a **tool**, not a ticket.

Never justify a low GPA. I recall an applicant I interviewed at Fort Lewis, Washington. When I asked about his low GPA, he said his priorities were simply in the wrong place. I said, "If you were to go back and do it over, would you do it differently?" He replied, "No, I don't feel I would." And, with that, I ruled him out. Here's the analogy I drew. A young man worked for me. I sent him out on a job to accomplish a given objective. Then, he came back with average to poor performance. We had a conversation as to why it could have been better. I asked him, "Now, if you had the opportunity to do that job again, would you do it differently?" He told me "No." I said, "You've got to be kidding." **So, be careful with suggesting that, in retrospect, you would still achieve only poor or fair performance**. **Never** defend poor performance.

We should **learn** as we grow older. Therefore, you wouldn't go back and do everything the same. We learn, for example, that the purpose of college is academics, not extracurricular activities. Square your shoulders and simply admit that you didn't accomplish what you had the capability of doing. You'd like the opportunity to go back and redo it. But, that's not possible — so, explain that you've been able to convert your low GPA into quality performance on the job. You're going to have to verbalize that. Most companies are not going to look at your officer evaluations, even though they may be your greatest asset.

Handle your GPA head-on. Don't back away from it. And, don't say you went to college to be "well-rounded"; therefore, your social life and extracurricular activities necessarily detracted from the effort you put on your studies. Let me tell you something. I've known many outstanding individuals with GPAs of 3.7 and higher. I can assure you they were extremely well-rounded. Don't suggest that because you have a low GPA, you're well-rounded, and the person with a high GPA is not. That's an alibi that will not stand up in the eyes of a recruiter. Don't explain away a low GPA. Confront it. It had to be either a question of poor judgment or a question of intellect. Let's hope it was the former.

Asking Quality Questions
A development candidate must show high intelligence in order to go to the top 10% of business. During your interview, the best indicators of your intellect are your curiosity and your questions. Let me repeat: **Ask quality questions.**

Asking questions during an interview is equally as important as your ability to answer questions. You will be judged on your intelligence, your comprehension of the job, the company, and the industry, your ability to express yourself, and the ability to ask a question that will get the information you need. Don't shrug this off. Don't think questions will come to mind when you get into an interview. I can tell you, questions don't come to you. You have to prepare **before** you go into the interview.

Don't ask vague, general questions or questions that will take more than approximately four minutes to answer. Make the questions precise and definitive. Do the necessary preparation to determine what, in fact, you need to know about a position in your chosen field.

During initial interviews, only ask questions related to the position you're seeking. If your questions are about benefits, locations, promotions and other irrelevant factors, you'll risk being eliminated. Take the position and break it down into its component parts. For sales positions perhaps the breakdown could include the following: product, customer, and bonus. For production: equipment, maintenance, and people. In an interview, focus on one part. All the questions you ask should relate to that part. Once you have exhausted this part, move on to another part.

One way to develop questions is to picture yourself backing out of your driveway on your way to a corporate job. Where are you going? What will you do when you get there? With whom? With what? For how long? Focus on the details of the position.

Try to get corporate literature prior to going into the interview. There is no better source for developing questions. Go into any interview with quality questions requesting information you **need** to make a decision. One of the best ways to do this is to take the literature that a company hands out and write down the questions as you read. If you don't do it that way, you might run into an extremely embarrassing situation asking a question that has been answered in the literature. This can be devastating to a quality interview. The recruiter says, "We print this literature which is $5 or $6 a brochure, and the applicant doesn't even have the professional courtesy to read it." In essence the applicant is saying, "I don't want to read the literature. I just want to go ahead and ask the questions." Be careful of that. Read the literature. It will prompt you to think of several relevant questions. Don't be **lazy**.

Your questions should never be **generic**, but must be company-specific. It is very impressive in your interview to show due diligence in your homework. For instance, the following remark shows the applicant did her research: "I was impressed as I read on pages two and three of your brochure, *Mobil Chemical Today*, how your president, Mr. Matos, was optimistic about your company's growth in the 1990s. Is that growth progressing on schedule?" You can see the positive impact this statement of fact (and something that could not be said to any other company) would make on a recruiter. When you do this, the question is being asked specifically for that company. Too many of you want to ask a question such as, "What is your turnover rate?" when you could say, "Obviously, at Mobil Oil, a quality company in the top 10 largest companies in America, you're very concerned about turnover. At Mobil, what is your labor force tenure?" Now, you have made it sound like a Mobil question. Before, it was simply generic. Don't be **lazy** about preparing questions.

Applicants have asked in interviews, "What new products are you bringing into the market?" They've got to be kidding. Companies will not take somebody off the street and tell them what they've got behind the wall. New products are the biggest secrets companies have. This kind of question shows poor judgment. Can you imagine going to the Iraqi Army and saying, "What new weapons are you developing?" They'd laugh at you. You're smart enough not to do that. You must also be smart when you interview with Corporate America.

You might find the words "one or two" useful in forming your questions. Here are good examples: "Could you tell me the two most frequent reasons for maintenance breakdown in your production line? Can you tell me the two most frequent reasons for turnover with your personnel?" In other words, by asking about one or two factors, you really are inquiring about the most frequent. We don't need to know all the reasons why people quit or why machinery breaks down, just the one or two reasons that are most important. So, you may find using "one or two" examples beneficial in asking quality questions.

For example, "How will I be evaluated in your company? In the military, I'm evaluated usually by two raters — my immediate rater and my senior rater. They evaluate on a host of different factors: my written and oral communications skills, my maturity, and knowledge of my job. I'm just curious. How do you evaluate employees of your company?" Take the time to design your question and formulate it (in relation to your historical background) so the recruiter can better address the question.

Be careful. Don't ask questions the recruiter will have to take 10 to 15 minutes of your 45-minute interview to answer. The recruiter is not going to accept you on the basis of his answers, but on the basis of **your** answers. While it is important for you to ask quality questions, it is also important to use good judgment in asking a question that can be answered in a concise, succinct manner.

Asking Negative Questions
Some of the questions you might ask are what we call negative questions, such as, "Could you give me insight into your turnover factor? Could you tell me about your safety program? Could you tell me about the tenure of your labor force? What percentage of your products are returned because of poor manufacturing quality? What percentage of your product is delivered to the customer on time?" These questions address

a point that may not be a positive selling point for the company. They must be asked in a manner that does not suggest you are a **cynical** person.

You need to turn the questions into positive questions. I recommend something like the following: "Obviously, a company of your quality is very concerned about its safety program. Could you give me some insight into your safety record?" or "I'm sure a company of your quality mandates the manufacturing of quality product. But, could you give me some insight into the percentage of product that is returned because of poor quality control?" The key is to make the tone of your questions positive. Take your time to develop questions. Word them so they are not negative.

In asking questions, do not use the word "type." "With what type people will I work?" Type means nothing. You must articulate your questions more precisely. Try to relate your question to the world in which you live. For example, "Obviously, a company of your quality has a very low turnover with its people. In the military, we have a very high turnover. It seems as if we (in many of our positions) have 100% to 110% turnover in a year. It isn't that I can't work with that and be effective, because I have proven I can, but could you give me some insight as to how it is in your company?"

I cannot express adequate concern over this issue of asking quality questions. Most applicants don't even think about it until it's too late. Just recently, I interviewed an applicant for 25 minutes of his 30-minute interview. I had previously stated at my information meeting that I would tell all applicants at the conclusion of their interview whether I could or could not support their move to Corporate America. At the end of 25 minutes and the end of my questions, I asked this applicant if he had questions. He said, "No, there is nothing

I can think of." So, I got up, opened the door, and let him out. I suppose he's still wondering if he was accepted. Should he read this book, he now knows he was not. But, can you really imagine someone filling out an application, leaving work, driving to my hotel, interviewing for 30 minutes, driving home, and **never** determining if he accomplished his objective. Wow! Never, ever suggest you don't have questions. Intelligent, curious people always have questions.

Sometimes, a recruiter will use most of the 45 minutes and end the interview. You have no time to ask any questions when the recruiters ask if you have any. **Be careful.** If you say "no," because in your mind the time is up, you'll be sending out a negative signal. On the other hand, if you say "yes," you do have questions, and now the recruiters have no time, they may not pursue you because of no time to answer your questions. A better way of handling it might be, "Yes, I have other questions, but nothing I need answers to at this time. I can already tell you, I have a very strong interest in your company, and I'll save my questions to be answered on my follow-up interview." **Be careful**. This is **only** if you're out of time. This is not a license not to ask questions. And, **never** make this statement of interest if it is not true.

I have also known recruiters who brought you in, sat you down, and stated, "Of course, you must have a thousand questions. Why don't you ask and I'll answer." This happens frequently, and you **must** be prepared for it.

I hope I've made my point. You must be serious about doing your homework and be prepared to ask quality questions. It's hard to get hired when you don't show intelligence, curiosity, and comprehension.

Colloquialisms And Qualifiers

Officers win the gold medal for using qualifiers. No one is as expert at using the qualifier as is the military officer. I have no idea where it comes from. "I think." "I believe." "Probably." You must understand that the minute you give any type of answer with a qualifier in it, your answer is immediately eliminated. What you've said to the recruiter is, "I'm not really sure, but here's what my guess would be." In an interview, we're not asking for your guess, we're asking for the way it **is**.

I remember I had a young recruiter working for me at one time. I had finally had it with him. We sat down and had a nose to nose conversation. I simply asked him what time it was. He looked at his watch and said, "I **think** it's **about** . . .," instead of looking at his watch and saying, "It's 1:09." In other words, he used two qualifiers just to tell me what time it was!

Do not use words such as "yeah," "you know," and "roger," or "check" for "yes." There is absolutely no reason for you to ever use the words "you know." I quickly remind the applicant that if "we knew," we wouldn't be asking the question.

I remember one individual who began every sentence with "okay" and ended with "okay." This is not something you can do and call yourself a good communicator. Be very careful of colloquial expressions and qualifiers.

Involving Spouses

Should spouses get involved? Absolutely. I'm very proud of the fact that in all the years I've been in this business, I have encouraged spouses to attend our information meetings and the Career Conferences. This is one of the most important moves you're going to make in your lifetime. Your career is probably the longest relationship next to marriage.

If you are married, you and your spouse should be examining this critical move as a team. Our information meetings include too many facts to take home to your spouse. Your spouse needs to get involved with you. After attending information meetings, he or she will have the ability to help critique your interview preparation. Spouses, be very honest in your critique. This is not the time to be nice or let things slide. If you do, when your spouse interviews with a recruiter, there is the tendency to say the same things. While frustrating for applicants, spouses must mention every time a word is misused. Point out when your spouse rambles, when they imply, but don't state, and when they say, "You know."

Ask yourself, "Do I understand exactly what my spouse is saying? Does my spouse come to the point immediately, give me substance, and answer the entire question? If I were a recruiter, would I like the way the answers were delivered? Is there enthusiasm in the voice and a sparkle in the eyes? Will my spouse excite the listener?" Detach yourself. Be a strict evaluator. Many spouses today have their own corporate careers or careers in engineering, teaching, sales, etc. They must be very demanding of a quality performance. It is the only way to help them improve themselves.

Talk into a tape recorder. You and your spouse can then better evaluate what you say. Sometimes, you will want to argue with your spouse, saying, "That isn't what I said," or "That isn't how I meant to say it," or "I don't think that's what I said." The tape recorder will play back exactly what you've said and won't lie to you. What you say is what it will say back to you. If you can't articulate into a tape recorder or deliver smoothly, you won't verbalize effectively in front of a recruiter either. These are frustrating methods of preparation, but frustration in front of your spouse, a tape recorder, or, for that matter, your recruiting firm will not cost you an interview.

Frustration in front of a company will probably cost you a follow-up interview and a job offer.

Working With Other Officers

Ask your recruiting firm what other officers from your base or post are coming to the same conference or conferences scheduled close together. **Work together.** Arrange an evening once a week when you can all get together to share questions and ideas and to critique each other. I do this frequently with my applicants. I find it extremely helpful. As you work with other officers, make a pact that you're going to be honest in critiquing one another. Be willing to throw out ideas. Be adventurous in responding to questions and different situations. There are many ways to prepare. If you'll work with other officers, it will force you to get out and do it. It will force you to think about it. While you may not want to embarrass yourself in front of other officers, those embarrassments and frustrations will cost you nothing. Where it will cost you is in front of a company.

Researching Companies

I'm frequently asked about the importance of doing research on companies before interviewing with them. If you're going to send out resumes and go into a company cold, you must research that company thoroughly. It's what we would call a nonstructured interview. So, you have absolutely no idea what it is the company is going to ask you during the course of the interview. For you not to have researched the company could spell trouble.

Check with your recruiting firm. It is usually unimportant and a waste of time to attempt to research a company prior to attending a given conference. Your recruiting firm should supply you with definitive information to cover the particular company, position, and recruiter. In fact, we supply our applicants with more pertinent information than they could find on their own in two weeks of research.

While this information is important, a successful interview is not based on what you know about the company, but rather on what you know about yourself. At our conferences, we have what we call structured interviews in which you communicate information about yourself. Many recruiters have said to me, "I don't really care what individuals know about us. I want to know what they know about themselves. What can they articulate to me in a concise manner in a 30- to 45-minute interview?" The research you need to do prior to a recruiting firm's conference is research on yourself. Have the ability to communicate that knowledge to a corporate recruiter.

Once a follow-up interview is scheduled, you must research that company thoroughly. Read the annual reports. Read the recruiting literature. Show an interest in the company. If it is a consumer-oriented company, go to a retail store and look at their product and how it's merchandised. If it is a tire company, go to a tire distributor and talk to them about the company's product. We like to see applicants who are resourceful enough to research the company in **unique ways** before their follow-up interview with that company.

If you're interviewing on your own, you don't have any idea what questions you are going to be asked. Therefore, you have no choice but to spend several hours researching that company prior to interviewing with them.

As you read corporate literature, highlight things of interest to you or points you want the company to clarify. Using a highlighter allows you to skim through the information in a matter of minutes. I also recommend you use 3 X 5 cards. Write questions on them, work on answers, and jot down notes of things you need to study.

Go to the business library to see if the company trades on one of the stock exchanges. If so, it will be easy for you to find corporate literature. If the company does not trade on one of the exchanges, call the company and ask them to send you literature. Tell them you are coming in for an interview and would like to read and study the literature ahead of time. There's nothing wrong with doing that. Attempt to find a couple of people who work for the company. Call them and have a conversation with them. Tell them again exactly what you're doing, that you will have an interview with the person- nel office on such and such a day and would like to get more information on the company. Having conversations with individuals who presently work for the company is better than all the literature you could read.

Recruiters have said to me, "Your applicants are extremely well prepared." I remember looking one recruiter in the eye and saying, "Of course, they are. Otherwise, you would be suggesting that they have a double standard." This is one of the most important steps that an applicant is ever going to take in life. Our applicants are the kind who are going to get their hands on every book they can. They talk with every recruiter they can. They learn the best way to have successful interviews. As a matter of fact, that's exactly the way compa- nies will expect people to approach an objective within their organizations. They will expect them to prepare well and to know everything there is to know about the objective they are attempting to accomplish. Applicants shouldn't set a double standard by not preparing well for interviews. The majority of applicants are ruled out because they **don't** prepare.

I even suggested to one recruiter that it is not my job to make his interviewing task easy by giving him people who don't know how to interview versus people who do. I suggested to the recruiter that it is his job to learn how to do a professional job of interviewing to determine exactly who the person is.

If recruiters suggest that you might be using someone else's answers, stop them right there. Let the recruiter know you have worked hard to be prepared. Yes, you have read interviewing handbooks — Roger Cameron's or other authors' handbooks. You've practiced and used tape recorders. Let the recruiter know the amount of work you've put in before the interview.

> ## DON'T USE MY WORDS.
> ## USE MY THOUGHTS.

Make sure the answers you give are your answers. They are very well thought out answers. They are prepared, but they're telling an accurate story of just who you are. Don't let any recruiter suggest that you should come to the marketplace unprepared. Appendix A provides additional information on definitions of critical characteristics for interview preparation.

Taking Time For Personal Development
I no longer ask my audiences if they have read *USA Today* or books that have been on the best seller list for months and months. For the most part, the military officer doesn't read. We're astonished! Let me tell you something. If you come to Corporate America, we want you to read. We want people who like to grow. We want people who have a high degree of

curiosity. We don't believe you're too busy to read. We don't believe you can't take a book to the field, or TDY, on an airplane, or in a vehicle with you.

Pick up a book for 30 minutes before going to bed at night. If you tell me, "I don't have time to do this," I think you need to honestly reevaluate your career and your life. You cannot spend the rest of your life in a formal academic environment. Therefore, you **must** read in order to rapidly gain knowledge. You cannot get through life without continuing to grow. My companies demand the hiring of growable, knowledgeable people.

Getting Organized

I've never observed a highly successful person who wasn't organized. Successful people are able to juggle numerous appointments, assignments, responsibilities, and dates to remember and still meet their obligations within difficult time limits. Learning to be thoroughly organized should be part of your early development. I see many military officers who do very well at this; however, many do not. Don't wait until others see you as unorganized and forgetful before you develop the professional habit of organizing and planning your time efficiently. I can attest to the fact that some development candidates have failed in their careers for just this reason.

I strongly recommend that you purchase a planning system. Two companies that have very good ones are:

• Day-Timers, Inc.
  One Day-Timer Plaza
  Allentown, PA 18195-1551
  1-800-523-9474

- Franklin International Institute
  P. O. Box 31406
  Salt Lake City, UT 84131-0406
  1-800-654-1776

In addition, there are many good software programs on the market that enable you to organize using your PC. Here are a few for you to explore:

- **On Time** (Campbell Services, Inc.)—This is a DOS version that is a combination appointment book, to-do list, pocket secretary, desktop planner, tickler file, and alarm clock. It graphically illustrates allocated time and lists undated items on the to-do list.

- **On Time for Windows** (Campbell Services, Inc.) — This system has the same features as On Time for DOS except that is uses the Windows interface.

- **1stACT** — 1stACT is easy to use and provides basic contact, calendar and to-do list management most needed to organize the day-to-day activity of computer users. Contact Software International. Available at CompUSA.

- **Lotus Organizer** — Lotus organizer is so easy to use because it works like a traditional paper organizer, then adds special Lotus features like Smarticons and mail capability. It's easy to organize daily planning, manage your time, and stay on top of contacts lists and notes. Lotus Development Corporation. Available at CompUSA.

- **Top Priority** (Power Up Software) — This software creates task and goal lists and prints to-do lists and reports to fit your personal organizer. You can merge all your lists into daily to-do lists so that large projects and goals appear as smaller achievable tasks each day. These tasks can be imported into Calendar Creator Plus to print out a graphical calendar.

Choosing Mentors

Choose at least two formal mentors as you enter Corporate America. The reason for selecting **two** or more mentors is because everyone has some biased opinions. It is good to have a balance of opinions to measure one suggestion against another. While both viewpoints may be accurate, combining the two opinions will give you confidence about the information you are receiving. I would recommend that you talk to your parents, friends, and contacts to identify people who have been successful in the business world. At least one of the mentors should work for a top *FORTUNE 500* company, if not both. I would suggest you select your mentors by the end of your first year in Corporate America, if not before. Choose these individuals very carefully. It is important for you to select people who have had successful careers and a level of experience that enables them to see the "big picture." If they are not successful, it will be difficult for them to give you the guidance and insight that will help you be successful.

Choose people to be your mentors who can give you quality information in a timely manner. I cannot imagine any successful corporate person who wouldn't be honored to give guidance to a young development candidate. Do not wait until important career decisions are thrust upon you before you seek out knowledgeable people to assist your thought process. Be proactive in establishing mentor relationships before you need them.

Many military officers often have a significant degree of naiveté about business. Recruiters today are more and more adamant about hiring people with good "street savvy" or business sense. Make a conscious effort to bring your corporate world business knowledge up to speed as quickly as possible. However, never count on a single source. As I mentioned several times in this book, continuing your formal education and having a vigorous reading program are very important.

The kind of mentors you want are extremely busy people. They are successful individuals. They are professionals with major corporations who make significant contributions to their companies — who accomplish difficult business objectives. Often, it is better for you to write them letters regarding questions you may have, or when you do call them, give them an option of two or three possible times they can speak with you. More than anything else, when you have received information, take the time to write a thank-you letter within 24 to 48 hours.

Let your mentors know what your strengths have been, what you like to do, and the extracurricular activities in which you participated during high school, college, and the military. Give them some insight as to what it is you want to accomplish in your life. Let them know what things excite you in a career. It is also helpful to be very candid about your financial status. Any advice given to you must be compatible with your personal financial situation. Prepare a resume and give copies to your mentors. The more information you can give them about yourself, the more accurate their insight and advice can be. I encourage you not to miss this critical activity of having mentors as you pursue a career in Corporate America.

Stop right now and set a deadline for selecting your mentors. Most successful people realize the advantage of mentorship and establish their mentors early in their career. Take action on this point.

Networking

Those in Corporate America have discovered the benefits of networking. Networking has become an art in itself. It involves establishing and maintaining relationships with people. It doesn't just happen. You must work at it. As an officer, you may know individuals in the corporate world — or you may not. You will find that most people enjoy helping others direct their careers and will talk to you and give you information. It's up to you to make the contacts. Look for opportunities with everyone you meet to develop relationships and to gather information on available jobs in their industries or companies.

During your military career, observe other outstanding officers who are establishing careers in Corporate America. Make their acquaintance, develop friendships, and most of all, maintain those friendships. Remember the law of maintaining relationships: "You must give as much or more than you receive." Think about what you have to offer other people that will contribute real value to their lives, and develop those capabilities. Too many people wait too late in life to appreciate the value of developing good relationships with others. As you move your career to Corporate America, I would suggest you develop your network in many different career paths, such as engineering, finance, data processing, accounting, and manufacturing. At any time in your career, you should be able to telephone a close friend who is employed as an engineer to discuss a technical issue or to call someone in finance to talk about financial analysis or financial planning for the future. I would recommend that you expand your network to include many companies and industries. This will provide you greater diversity of knowledge.

Developing A Master Mind Group

Another excellent way to network is to form a "master mind" group. Many executives and entrepreneurs are members of master mind groups. Members meet periodically to brainstorm solutions to issues of importance. The master mind principle makes it possible for an individual, through association with others, to acquire the knowledge of those individuals without having their education level. For example, an engineer can explain a technical principle perfectly, but you don't need a four-year engineering degree to understand it. The master mind concept suggests that there is more opportunity for success in dealing with obstacles to a goal if two or more minds work in perfect harmony toward that goal.

Scarcely a day goes by that we aren't gaining information from diverse, educated, and knowledgeable people, and understanding it — without an equal amount of education. Most of us go through life having non-formal master mind alliances, usually in an unconscious state of mind. I'm suggesting you formalize your own master mind group.

I belong to two master mind groups. I regret waiting until I was 55 years old to become a member. I have received many direct benefits, allowing me to save many hours of frustration and to accomplish some personal goals more quickly and more efficiently. I hope at the same time I have contributed to others in my groups. Don't put the master mind idea on a back burner. Take advantage of the synergy gained from such an alliance.

One of the major goals of a corporate master mind group should be to help the members do as much as possible to improve their opportunities to have successful careers. For example, your group may want to address specific career opportunities in your field and discuss how members of the group can achieve higher performance.

Be selective about who will be a member of your group. Choose people with similar interests, who have the intelligence and enthusiasm to contribute significantly to the group, and who have been successful in the past. Select people from all geographical areas and career paths. Friends may or may not be appropriate choices. Consider inviting alumni from your college who have worked in Corporate America to be members, keeping in mind that those individuals must see value in being part of the group.

> **Early in your career, it is what you know;**
> **then, it becomes who you know;**
> **finally, it changes to who knows you.**

Your group may want to invite people in industry to speak on topics of importance to you and, afterwards, to answer questions from the group. Consider pooling resources and hiring training consultants who deliver business seminars to instruct your group. The opportunities are endless. The point is that, as a group, you have exciting ideas to explore.

If, for some reason, any individuals do not fit in the group, be firm about asking them to drop their membership. The key is to have an extremely compatible, supportive group, with members who are enthusiastic about meeting the objectives of the group.

If you are the leader of the group, be sure to maintain a positive attitude at all times. Your responsibility is to help the other members maintain a lively interest in being supportive and cooperative.

Your group can be as large or as small as you like. The larger the group, the longer you need to meet so that everyone can have time to contribute. Establish a specific time each week, every two weeks, or monthly for the meeting. Development candidates have busy schedules during the day. Trying to set up meetings during this time will be difficult. Try early morning (6:30 A.M.) or late in the evening (9:30 P.M.) when most of the members might be able to attend.

Appendix B lists books I recommend for your personal development. This list is not exhaustive, but suggests magazines, newspapers, and business books to help you prepare for corporate interviews.

Appendix C provides numerous adjectives that will help you determine your behavioral traits.

**THE SECRET OF SUCCESS IS DOING
WHAT YOU OUGHT TO DO,
WHEN YOU OUGHT TO DO IT,
WHETHER YOU WANT TO OR NOT,
NO DEBATE.**
— Walter Hailey, Jr.

CHAPTER 4

The Physical Factors Of Interviewing

"With Roger's help, I was able to get a job that is normally reserved for business school graduates from Harvard, Stanford, and Wharton. He demands and gets high standards from his applicants. There are many young executives in Corporate America who have Roger to thank for their opportunity to enter industry."

— Kevin Corning
Brand Manager
Kraft General Foods

CHAPTER 4

The Physical Factors Of Interviewing

Being On Time

Few behaviors can hinder your climb to the top of the corporate ladder more than being late when you make commitments. When you are late in arriving for an event or appointment, in accomplishing an objective, in turning in a report, or in sending a thank-you note, the impression you leave is less than satisfactory. Make it a habit — never be late.

I encourage you to look at being late for an interview from the point of view of a recruiter. Often, when you are late, you are thinking, "I'll only be a minute late — or, at the most, five minutes late." I encourage you to realize you are the only one who knows this. The person expecting you knows nothing. When you are late by even a minute, the recruiter is placed in the uncomfortable position of wondering where you are. Numerous possibilities present themselves — perhaps you are in the elevator, maybe you have forgotten the appointment, or perhaps you've even had an accident. As the minutes go by, the recruiter doesn't know whether to wait, make a phone call, or leave to do other work. In any case, your action has resulted in the recruiter wasting time. After you force a recruiter's anxiety level to climb, it may be difficult for you to get an objective interview.

The message is this: Consider what being late says about you — **nothing good!**

Clothes And Appearance

Once you start to work for a company, you'll be measured primarily according to your performance. When you interview, you're going to be judged on every possible factor, including what you wear. It's sad to hear of someone who has worked hard to secure a good education, spent money to build a resume, put in time preparing for interviews, and is ruled out because of the way he or she is dressed.

If you're outstanding and have done everything right, it's possible, but doubtful your clothes will rule you out of a job — unless they are unprofessional. But, if the recruiter feels something about you is questionable and that is compounded by a poor appearance, then your clothes will become a major factor. I recommend that you read John Molloy's *Dress For Success* (for men or women). Acceptable business attire for men has been established and widely practiced for many years. On the other hand, business attire for women is not universally understood, and women can easily make serious mistakes when they take advice from well-meaning people (even clothing store personnel) who do not understand what constitutes professional business clothing for women. Therefore, it is very important for women to read Mr. Molloy's *Dress For Success For Women*. The best rule of thumb for men and women to remember regarding appearances in the entire interviewing and hiring process is this:

> Your physical appearance should imply that you are professional and competent and that you can get the job done. This does not mean you should look dull, but if you err, it should be on the side of being conservative versus highly fashionable. Remember, you are not trying to please your friends or the fashion experts, but rather the people who make hiring decisions. These individuals are usually older and conservative (at least

in their business appearance), and care more about what you can accomplish than how good-looking you are.

We recommend that women applicants have two suits for interviewing purposes. Each should have matching jacket and skirt and should be designed in a traditional style, in solid colors of either navy blue or gray. Some national brands we recommend are Austin Reed, Cricketeer, and Jones of New York. Many styles and colors are available in women's business suits today, and you must select suits of traditional cuts and colors for interviewing. Women should not wear pin stripe suits or men's ties or try to look like men. The length of the skirt should be just below the knee to two inches below the knee. White or off-white tailored blouses are best. They should not be sheer, overly lacy, or made of a fabric commonly worn in social situations. The neckline should be discreet and professional in appearance.

Shoes should be low-heeled (two inches or less is a good rule of thumb) with closed toes and heels. You should be able to stand easily and walk briskly in your shoes. Black, navy, or other dark neutral colors are best. Wear natural-colored hose with no seams or texture.

A woman's handbag should be of small or moderate size and only large enough to carry essentials. It should be what we call "a business purse" that simply gets the job done. Again, black, navy, or dark neutral colors are best.

These points are also important for women: Keep your jewelry to a minimum for an interview. One ring on each hand (at the most) and a strand of pearls or a simple gold chain is sufficient jewelry. If you wear earrings, they should be small or fit close to the earlobe. Dangling earrings are not appropriate.

Women should have a hairstyle that is neat and professional. If your hair is below shoulder length, wear it pulled back — in a chignon or French braid. A tailored hairstyle is best.

Your make-up should be light — blush and lipstick that are natural-looking rather than bright or dramatic. Avoid heavy eyeliners or shadows. Your fingernails should be medium to short in length. If you wear nail polish, be sure it is clear. Keep perfume light or wear none at all.

For both men and women, the rule is to look conservative, professional, and classic. Everything should be done in moderation. That's why overdoing perfume or aftershave lotion can leave a reminder of you long after you're gone — and **not** in a positive way.

I have no idea why anyone would come to an interview wearing an alarm clock — whether it's a Big Ben you put up on the recruiter's desk or a wristwatch you wear on your arm. If I'm in the middle of an interview and the applicant's alarm clock goes off, it is very disrupting. I consider it very unprofessional. If you need a watch that tells you every time the hour or the half-hour strikes, that's just fine, but turn it off or remove it before you come to an interview.

While a recruiter for a major national company was interviewing an applicant, the applicant's wristwatch went off. The recruiter got up from behind his desk and said, "Obviously, you have something more important than this interview," walked the young man to the door, and let him out. I don't blame him. It's highly inconsiderate to take an alarm clock with you to an interview.

In stressing very light jewelry for all male applicants, I suggest nothing more than a class ring, a wedding band, and a business-style wristwatch.

Men's hair should be cut in a conservative, professional style. If you have partible hair, then part it. If your hair is very fine and has a tendency to blow out of shape with the slightest breeze, then use hair spray to hold it in place. And, watch out for the strange things a hat or cap can do to your hair. When you remove a hat or cap, be sure your hair is combed and well-groomed.

Men should also have two suits. Each should be two-piece and single-breasted with one and one half-inch cuffs on the pants. One suit should be navy blue and the other dark gray with a subtle, single, three-fourths inch gapped, white pin stripe. The stripe should be very discreet and only visible when you are within arm's length.

It's critical that you buy two suits for your job search. Then, you won't get stuck in a situation that can often occur. For example, the company representative with whom you are interviewing meets you at the end of your flight and you both go to dinner. You must wear the suit you wore while traveling. That means the next day this suit will not be acceptable in appearance for your interview. You **must** have the second suit.

Your suits don't need to be extremely expensive, but they should be of good quality. There are several good brands, but one we consistently recommend is Hart, Schaffner & Marx. This company sells good quality, inexpensive business suits and knows exactly what you need in a business cut. Often, you can find two suits on sale for the price of one that are acceptable for interviews. Your suits should always be extremely well-pressed for interviews.

Your shirts should be white with button-down collars. I usually suggest 100% cotton. Many business people who are constantly on the road have to send out their shirts to hotel laundries. Let me assure you that if you travel the circuit I travel, you won't be able to wear 99% of the shirts returned from these laundries. One side of the collar goes one way, the other another way. That's why you should wear shirts with button-down collars. Don't assume that the shirts you send to the laundry will be ironed satisfactorily. A typical scenario is that you get your laundry back at 7:00 P.M. Your interview is at 7:00 A.M. the next morning. You wear the shirt the way it is — or you don't wear it. You have no choice. The button-down design overcomes any collar problem caused by a laundry.

Your ties should be "power ties" — bold in color — so that they are the focal point. There's a very simple reason for this. When you travel, you can't take four or five suits with you and change your suit frequently. If you want to switch your tie in the middle of the day, 90% of those around you will think you've changed your entire suit.

You can't buy a $15 tie today that's acceptable for an interview. You will need to spend $30 or more. Don't ruin an interview for the sake of saving $10 or $15.

Wear good-quality socks that are over-the-calf, such as socks from Brooks Brothers. You can run in these socks, and they will stay up. Don't wear socks that bunch down around your ankles, as I so often see in interviews.

The shoe I recommend is a wine-colored, wing-tipped cordovan with a tassel. When you travel, you can't carry a lot of different shoes. You can wear the shoe I recommend with a tan, brown, black, or blue suit. It's an extremely acceptable shoe and is a good choice for interviews and casual wear. Be sure your shoes are well-shined. There is no excuse for any other appearance. There are even small shoeshine kits available that you can carry in your pocket.

Occasionally, a recruiter will tell you to wear casual clothes for dinner or hiring sessions other than the actual interview sessions. But what does that mean? There is no official definition of casual clothes. For men, I recommend quality slacks, a shirt, a tie, and a sport jacket. (A suit jacket worn with slacks is **not** a sport jacket.) For women, I recommend a skirt and blouse with a blazer or a dress — not pants.

As a male, if you find your male dinner companion isn't wearing a jacket or a tie, it's very simple to remove yours. It's easy to dress down, but impossible to dress up. Let me assure you that if you are in an interview and you're under-dressed, you can't make up the difference there. Know ahead of time what will be expected of you. If you are not advised by the company with which you are interviewing, ask what is appropriate.

Remember, what you wear when you go to work for a company will be at your own discretion within their professional set of standards. You'll be measured primarily on your work performance, but in the job search, your clothes are a key factor that companies use to evaluate your judgment.

Glasses

Sunglasses should never be worn in an interview. Recruiters want to see your expression and have eye contact with you. It is very difficult, if not impossible, to see through tinted glasses. Some of you wear the photogrey glasses that change with sunlight. The unfortunate thing is that, many times, when you come into a hotel or any interview environment, you will sit next to a window. Photogrey will automatically tint the glass. These glasses are perfectly all right to work in under certain circumstances, but they are not the best for interviewing.

I also recommend that when you purchase glasses, you choose professional frames that will be appropriate with the clothes you wear to your interviews. The easiest way to be sure your selection is a good one is to wear one of your interview suits and try on the frames in front of a full-length mirror.

Most importantly, have your glasses fitted professionally so that you won't have to push your glasses into place repeatedly during the interview. Applicants often have developed such a habit of doing this that they make the motion of pushing their glasses into place even when they are not wearing them! Most optometrists will adjust your glasses free of charge while you wait. Therefore, take advantage of this service and make sure your glasses fit properly.

Posture
Often, you must sit in chairs which contribute to poor posture. Sometimes, the arm rests are positioned in a way that you cannot help but rest your elbows on them. When you do, your hands are up in your face. I've seen applicants come in and talk through their hands, actually leaning on their hands at 9:00 A.M. as if they were tired.

Posture is important. Sit up straight in the chair. **Control** your environment — don't let the environment control **you**. You can change your posture. Don't sit there as stiff as a board. We call that "military stiff." Be natural — but with good posture. And, it's okay to cross your legs.

Don't sit on the front edge of a chair or couch. Sit **back** in the chair so that when you want to emphasize a point, you can lean forward and stress that point. If you're sitting on the edge of your chair, when you lean forward, you may fall off. I've actually had this happen to applicants. It's embarrassing for both of us. We're always looking for **professional** enthusiasm, not **nervous** enthusiasm. The first is comfortable. The second eventually makes even the recruiter nervous. We like high energy — but, we don't want it to drive us out of the room.

Chewing Gum

This is an automatic rule out. I'm always disappointed when an officer steps in front of me in an interview, at an information meeting, or at a conference attempting to communicate with me while chewing gum. It's rude and unprofessional. When I've ruled applicants out for this reason and explain why, they are always quick to tell me they would never chew gum in front of a company. You've got to be kidding! Now, you're telling me you are simply selectively unprofessional! Please, never have anything in your mouth as you talk to others.

Smoking

Here's the rule on smoking — **never**, during an interview. Never. If you smoke, then smoke before you go to your breakfast, lunch, or dinner meeting, but do not smoke during an interview. When you're hired, it may be acceptable to smoke on the job or at least in designated smoking areas. However, more and more companies are hiring the non-smoker.

Foul Language

There can **never** be an excuse to use foul language in an interview, or, for that matter, anywhere in Corporate America. What you're saying is that you do not have the ability to express your point of view without it. If you do that, you're really telling Corporate America everything they want to know about you. Our world is not a perfect world. I've actually had to talk to some recruiters who use four-letter words in interviews. I see absolutely no excuse for it and always feel sorry for a person who has to communicate using that type of language. Do yourself a favor and never bring foul language to an interview.

Nervous Habits

You should be able to come into an interview, regardless of the environment, and concentrate specifically on what you are doing. I've seen interviews take place in almost every location possible — bathrooms, hallways, parking lots, hotel rooms, or on a walk around the block.

Control the interviewing environment. Don't let nervous habits unconsciously make you look bad. Focus.

For example, in some hotels, the room where the interview takes place has a window that looks out on the swimming pool. I've had applicants indicate they're more interested in checking out what's happening pool-side than they are in focusing on the interview. If you're looking out the window at traffic on the street, you're losing vital concentration.

I've known recruiters who will purposely try to distract you. They may turn on the TV, without sound, to see if you can still focus on the interview rather than on the TV screen. If you don't have the ability to go into an environment and focus on the reason for being there, you won't accomplish your objective.

Many officers insist on fiddling with those government pens all of you seem to carry. There you are, during an interview —

fiddling, as if it didn't mean anything, as if it didn't reveal an unconscious nervous habit. Another nervous habit is waving one leg back and forth when one leg is crossed over the other. I had one applicant who did this constantly, so I suddenly took my left arm and began waving it back and forth from my shoulder out. I continued to ask questions. The applicant stared at me. I asked, "Am I bothering you?" He said, "Yes, you really are." I then pointed out his nervous habit which had been distracting me. He sat very still for the balance of the interview and became conscious of a subconscious nervous habit. You may say, "I would never do that." I have seen many people with nervous habits. When I brought it to their attention, they were not even conscious they had been doing something. So, this isn't something that just happens to a few people or the unfortunate few people. It happens to a lot of people. Be very careful of it.

Sometimes, I want to say to an applicant, "Would you mind **sitting** on your hands?" Almost every second they're attempting to communicate with their hands. It's okay to do that on occasion. But, in the interview, you must do everything in moderation. You can't talk with your hands throughout an interview. It gets annoying — and we try to imagine you at a staff meeting. It becomes so distracting that it's difficult to concentrate on what you're saying.

Many hotels have noisy window air conditioning units. But, sometimes, applicants will ignore the noise. They'll still talk in a normal tone of voice instead of lifting their voices to overcome the air conditioning. If I have to turn off the air conditioning in order to hear the applicant, I'm going to reject him or her. If they're not aware enough to raise their voice over the noise, then they're really not the kind of person my companies are paying me to find.

Also, there's the problem of what some people do with their rings. I've had applicants take off a wedding band and try it on each finger, not even aware of what they're doing. One man got his ring stuck on his thumb and had a hard time getting it off. Another put both little fingers in the wedding band. They got stuck, and I had to hold the wedding band in place, so this individual could pull his fingers out.

When a ring falls to the floor, it invariably rolls under the bed, under the couch, or under the table. It's embarrassing — you're sitting there in your good-looking two-piece suit. Then, suddenly, you're on the floor, trying to retrieve a ring from under the bed.

Watch your nervous habits. Don't stare out the window, gesture constantly with your hands, or fiddle with your wedding band. It's amazing how many applicants can be totally unaware of doing these things.

What To Take To An Interview

When you go to an interview, take a pen and spiral notebook that are **small** enough to fit into your suit coat pocket. Make sure your pen is noise-proof and has no parts that click when you nervously hold it. You will use the notebook to take down an address (if a company wants you to send them something) or a phone number if the recruiter wants you to call him or her. You should pull out your notebook when you are introduced to someone and write down the individual's name. I know how frequently you are introduced to someone, and this helps you remember.

If they are wearing a name tag, that is different. You can look at the name tag and have it remind you. Otherwise, do not be embarrassed about pulling the notebook out of your pocket and writing down the individual's name — particularly if you get into an interview where there are several recruiters. It's critical to write their names down to be able to remember them and to also send them thank-you letters later. Do not be afraid to ask them how to spell their names for clarification: "Tim? Or, did you say Jim?" There is absolutely nothing wrong with that. I know of many embarrassments where people have forgotten names. You shouldn't walk into the interview with the pad in your hand; it should be readily accessible. It should be clean so you don't have to thumb through pages finding a page to make a note on it. When you're through making notes on a particular company, remove the sheet from the notebook. Then, as you go into your next interview, you can again be prepared to write on a clean page.

I strongly recommend you go through self-evaluation after **every** interview. See interviewing points in Appendix D.

CHAPTER 5

Understanding Interviewing Techniques

"One of the most difficult aspects of the career transition is gaining the knowledge of the process. Roger is known for his complete attention to detail and total professionalism. Through Roger, the doors to several quality opportunities were opened for me. He was there then as a counselor and coach, and he is there now as a friend and advisor."

— Jim Morse
Director of
Corporate Accounts
Deknatel, Inc.

CHAPTER 5

Understanding Interviewing Techniques

Time To Verbalize

Military officers have a phenomenon in their backgrounds called "moving to the next step based on the observation of past performance."

You go to grade school. You're observed by your teachers. At the end of that observation period, they grade you. Based upon those grades, you take the next step by moving on to junior high. Based on observation and grades, you go on to high school. The procedure follows you into college, then into ROTC, and then into the military.

You are observed and graded. You then take the next logical steps. However, when you leave the military, and make the decision to go into business, you must **verbalize** these past successes. You're not afforded the opportunity to be **observed** before being graded — the observation is based upon how you verbalize success in the interview. No other point makes more military officers fail. You have never had to verbalize past accomplishments or your leadership style. You haven't practiced doing so. This is absolutely a critical point: Verbalize your accomplishments and record them into a tape recorder. I can assure you that whatever you **give** that tape recorder, it will give you **back**. When you listen to the recording, be honest. Ask yourself the following questions: Did I communicate in an articulate fashion? Was I concise? Did I say what I wanted to say and conclude the subject matter? Did I address the question directly? It is unfortunate that so many military officers who have been good performers in the past do not have the ability to verbalize that performance. They therefore have been ruled out by industry for positions as development candidates.

No company will come out and observe you in the Army (say for a period of five months), then, if they like what they see, give you an offer. You have to describe your success in a series of interviews for probably the first time in your life.

Communicating in Common Sense English

In order to communicate effectively to Corporate America, you must admit to yourself that you presently speak in a "military language" of acronyms. You cannot communicate intellectually using terms such as boat, NTC, platoon, unit, battalion, company, TDY, down range, and many more. If you would like to test me, go to most street corners in America, stop the first 10 people and ask them some questions. "Which is larger: platoon, company, unit, or battalion? How many personnel are in a platoon, a company, and a unit? What is the function of a platoon, a company, and a unit?" Too many military officers simply are lazy in communicating. In the military, you all understand these terms. You can "read between the lines" and, in many cases, finish one another's sentences. However, recruiters can't and wouldn't if they could. They require you to be able to express yourself accurately.

We would expect to hear an exchange as follows. "My armor platoon of 18 soldiers and 5 tanks was part of an 85-soldier armor company. During our annual gunnery evaluation, which graded our ability to fire on both stationary and moving targets, we qualified with the highest score out of the 4 companies in our 300-soldier battalion."

Frankly, you have it right when you can call Grandma or Grandpa and have them understand what you're saying. Usually, after you tell them what you do, they'll change the subject to, "Well, that's wonderful, and how's your spouse?" In other words, they want to get the subject over to something they can understand. Recruiters just decline you.

Evading A Question
Never evade a question. When a recruiter asks a specific question, answer it. Listen carefully to the question and be certain you understand it so that you do not appear to evade it. For example, if the question is, "What is your location preference?" don't reply that you are open, but rather give a preference which is regional, such as the Southeast or the Northwest. State it in the broadest of terms — for example, "east of the Mississippi River."

A question that calls for a "yes" or "no" should **immediately** be answered with the words "yes" or "no," and then you may support it. Too often, when I ask a particular question, the applicant replies with a lot of rhetoric, and I must sit there and wonder if this is going to lead to a "yes" or a "no." Have the self-confidence to say "yes" or "no" immediately and then support your answer. When that individual sitting in front of me says, "Yes," and then supports it, I know exactly where we're going. I don't have to question or wonder. I don't have to remember all the rhetoric to determine the answer.

Spontaneous And Reflective Questions
You will be asked two types of questions in an interview: spontaneous and reflective. **Spontaneous** questions take about 5% of any interview. Examples include the following: How do you pronounce your last name? Where did you go to college? What was your grade point average? What was your major? Where is your home town? Obviously, these answers

are on the tip of your tongue, and you can quickly, spontaneously answer them.

The most frequently asked question is the **reflective** question. You must cover these four basic steps in responding:

1) **Listen.** Actively listen to each word the interviewer puts into a sentence.

2) **Reflect.** Think about the question. How will you answer?

3) **Organize** the answer in your mind.

4) **Deliver** your answer.

I might add a fifth step — knowing when to **"shut up."** Too many people continue to talk, when, in fact, they have already given the answer.

Not listening is the number one reason officers are eliminated from an interview. You must understand exactly what the recruiter is asking, then address the question directly. As the recruiter asks you a question, give an indication that you are listening with a nod of your head or a movement of your eyes. Let the recruiter feel that you are eagerly listening to everything. Also, be sure you don't attempt to show signs of wanting to answer the question before the recruiter is even finished. That displays very poor manners. You should never answer a question until you have heard the complete question. Some applicants make me feel I actually need to stop asking the question because, in some magical way, they have been able to read my mind. I know they haven't, but they make me feel that way. Listen intently. Show signs of listening. Do not attempt to respond before the recruiter is finished. Focus. Focus. Focus.

When you're asked a **reflective** question, it's perfectly all right for you to take three, four, or even five seconds to think. This is much better than restating the question. Please don't do that. It suggests that the recruiter lacked the ability to articulate. The reason you normally restate the question is just because you want two or three seconds to think. It is perfectly all right to simply take a few quiet seconds to reflect.

You should always be as spontaneous as you can. But, you should never be spontaneous to the point of hurting yourself. Avoid the danger of talking, then thinking, then ending up rambling. Recruiters will give you a lot more credit for a few seconds of silence — and then a well-delivered answer — than for being spontaneous, and, therefore, inadequate with a **reflective** answer.

It is also very important to deliver your answer smoothly. Too frequently, applicants begin their answer, stop, rethink, reorganize, redeliver, begin again, and go back to the analysis. Take the time to think through the answer you want to give. It will be critical for you to deliver in a fluid manner.

Today, the effective use of time is becoming more and more critical as companies assign people more responsibility. Industry wants to see that work is done in an eight- to nine-hour day — instead of adding hours to complete the job. We're looking for people who use time effectively — people who work "smart." So, an interviewer wants to see if you have a logical, organized mind. The recruiter wants to discover during the 35- to 45-minute interview whether or not you **organize your answers**. Do you maximize the amount of interviewing that can be done in the time period? We're looking for people who use time effectively — who work smart. In other words, we look for those people who are **peak performers**, not workaholics.

Evaluating Your Answer
Your answer will be evaluated in three ways, regardless of who is asking the question.

- **First,** the **substance** or content of your answer.

  - Did you give a **complete** answer?
  - Did the interviewer have to ask two or three questions to get a full reply?
  - Are you able to convey a complete thought/make your point?
  - Do you find people misinterpret you?

- **Second,** the **articulation** you use — how you say it. Deliver your answer so that your audience understands exactly what your point of view is. Frequently, an officer will forget the question — or go off on a tangent, misusing the interview time — and give irrelevant information.

  - How **expressive** is your voice?
  - Do you use proper intonation, voice volume, facial expression, and **verbal enthusiasm** as you talk?
  - Do you have the ability to get someone else to respond to your ideas or thoughts because of your enthusiasm — do you excite?
  - Can you make your point without being abrasive, combative, or abrupt?
  - Do you emphasize key words?
  - Do you mumble?
  - Are you sensitive to the impact of your voice? If you scream, people tend to scream back. If you whisper, they whisper back. Be aware of this and begin to **notice what affect your voice has on others and how effective your voice can be.**

- **Third,** the **succinctness,** or conciseness, of your answer. Give answers with as few words as possible — but deliver substance. Being succinct is a trait that officers are not conscious of since the military will extend an eight-hour day to get the job done. In Corporate America, however, the employee must have the ability **to accomplish maximum tasks in minimum time.**

Use the following exercises to critique your articulation and speech patterns.

Exercise #1
Prepare an answer to the request, "Tell me about yourself." This is a very common interview question. You need to explain or present your background to an interviewer in a clear and concise manner. An interview is a **conversation** with the interviewer. Therefore, be very careful not to come across as though you are giving a canned answer or speech. Your discussion about yourself should be sincere and natural.

Have your spouse and/or a friend listen to your answer — or record it on a tape recorder. Concentrate on speaking clearly and enunciating your words. Be aware of your voice projection, and yet, be sensitive to your impact on the other person.

- Are you speaking too loudly — too softly?
- Do you drop the volume of your voice at the end of sentences?
- Do you talk too quickly?
- Do you slur your words together?
- Do you talk slower than is normal for a conversation?
- Are you picking your words too carefully?

Have the other person critique you, and, if you have used a tape recorder, critique yourself.

Exercise #2

Prepare a **speech** on a subject of importance to you. Present this speech to your spouse or a friend **and** record it on tape. The purpose of this exercise is to reveal to you how your speaking pattern varies when you give a speech versus when you are carrying on a conversation. In an interview, it is very important for you to be conversational, natural, and sincere — you should NOT sound like you are giving a speech. Listen to the tape recording of your speech. Compare it to the tape of your reply in Exercise #1. You should notice the differences in your speaking patterns. Do not fall into "giving a speech" in an interview.

It is very important for you to use this criteria as you practice and evaluate your tape recorded answers. Be sure that your spouse or friend understands these points, so he or she can also use them in critical evaluation of your answers. It's better to be frustrated with yourself prior to being in an interview versus being mad at yourself after an interview — when you find out you were ruled out because you didn't deliver substance in an articulate, natural, and concise manner.

Frequent Mistakes

Over the many years corporate recruiters have interviewed my applicants, I have asked them to provide feedback on each applicant they interviewed and their reasons for acceptance or decline. This feedback has reached into the thousands and reveals the three most frequent reasons a military officer gets eliminated during interviews.

1) **Doesn't listen**. A recent study published by a major periodical (which requires strong proof and evidence for any article they print) showed that top managers in Corporate America spend 73% of their time listening. Therefore, if during the first 30 minutes of communication with a company

you prove your lack of ability to listen, you can imagine how that influences the decision to hire you as a development candidate. Often, an officer will listen to the overall question, but fail to listen to **each word**. Thus, the answer may be incomplete. If you can't listen properly, then recruiters will understandably be concerned about your skill in communicating. Applicants have often left an interview thinking they have had a great interview when, in fact, they were not even addressing the questions asked. Instead of talking "apples," they were talking "oranges."

2) **Doesn't excite**. Excitement generally comes from your verbal ability to communicate — your verbal enthusiasm, the inflection of your voice, how you walk, and your handshake.

3) **Rambles**. Rambling means you didn't organize your answer, didn't have confidence in it, and didn't think it out. You must think, and then talk, or your answer won't have substance. Too frequently, what you're doing is talking — and then thinking.

Don't ignore these three frequent mistakes. Write them on the cuff of your shirt or the palm of your hand. Don't get casual about these three points. Again and again, companies cite these as the most common reasons to rule out an applicant. If you read nothing else in this book, and avoid only these mistakes, you will then be head-and-shoulders above most applicants interviewing coast to coast. More recruiter comments on mistakes are discussed in Chapter 7.

High Energy Level
Companies come to me and say, "Don't bring me applicants who are tired. We want people with **high energy**." In a corporate sense, high energy means the ability of an individual

to put out as much work the eighth hour of the day as he or she does in the first hour of the day. After all, people are paid as much for the last hour as for the first hour.

In an interview, we measure high energy in three ways.

1) **Visible high energy — how you walk.** Do you demonstrate a sense of urgency? A favorite recruiter of mine at Texas Instruments likes to stand outside his door about five minutes before the time of an interview so that he can see the applicant turn the corner down the hall. If the applicant doesn't pick up their pace between the back of the hall and the interviewer's door, they are on the downhill side before stepping into the office. Recruiters want to see that you have energy in the way you walk. Keep in mind that you may be observed outside the office where you are interviewed. Maintain a lively pace no matter where you are.

2) **Feeling of high energy — handshake.** When you shake hands, it should be purposeful. You should step **into** the **handshake,** whether it's with a man or a woman. The handshake should be firm — full into the hand, showing a physical demonstration of high energy rather than strength. Energy should flow from **you** to the person with whom you're shaking hands.

3) **Audible high energy — enthusiasm in your voice.** Recruiters want to hear the energy in your voice. Does your voice convey excitement and eagerness for the work with changes in its tone and pitch?

I remember listening to a professor of military science talk to an ROTC group at a major southern college. He had a strong voice and delivery. But, I noticed that he turned his audience off about five minutes into his speech. They were looking at the floor, out the windows, and at their books and papers. At first, I couldn't understand why his audience was paying so little attention to him. Then, I realized he had absolutely no voice inflection. His voice was booming, but everything came out in a monotone. He didn't **modulate** his voice.

Verbal enthusiasm and voice inflection should go hand in hand. Too often, companies say to me, "Roger, the applicant said the correct things, but not in a convincing manner."

Making Things Happen

I was in Colorado Springs speaking with an Air Force officer whom I had just declined. I asked the young man if there was any insight or help I could give him. He said, "Mr. Cameron, could you tell me in one sentence what it is that recruiters are looking for most in a development candidate?" It almost made me think I had made a mistake in declining him. I replied that recruiters are simply looking for an individual who can **make things happen** — who is goal-oriented and success-driven. Corporations don't want to hire people who feel it is satisfactory to fail as long as they have an excuse. Typical excuses include the following: "Oh, I'm sorry I'm late. I didn't know it was going to rain." "I didn't know Sally was going to take off for four weeks of vacation." "I didn't know the parts were going to come in late." "I didn't know my car was going to have a flat tire." "I didn't know." Too many employees feel as long as they have an excuse, it is all right to fail. Recruiters disagree. They are looking for people who have the ability to find solutions to problems and make them successes. They must see that you have the ability and desire to overcome adversity.

Look around in the military. Aren't there some people you know who have a tremendous ability to **make things happen**? Those individuals are goal-/mission-oriented and the kind of people we're looking for. As you come to Corporate America, many times you will be faced with difficult objectives. There are people who throw up their hands and quit when the going gets difficult. This is not the kind of person who would be considered a development candidate going to the top of a major corporation. The best compliment I can hear is, "He/she is a make-it-happen type person." I will admit that certain people have the ability to do it and others don't. It is one of the reasons I have to interview so many people in a year to find the types we want. It's like the individual who interviews with me and has five officer evaluations — all average. Interestingly enough, none of them were her fault! In each case, she was a victim of circumstance. We may think this can happen on occasion. But, if every rater, perhaps five different ones, come up with the same conclusion — there's little doubt as to what our decision is going to be in this situation.

I remember a young man in El Paso, Texas, who had an appointment with me at 6:00 P.M. He arrived at the door 15 minutes late. As I went to the door, he said, "I'm sorry I'm late; the traffic was bad." I didn't even ask him to come in and sit down. It was obvious to me this individual thought nothing of being late because he had an excuse. I really don't know of any place, including Fredericksburg, Texas, that the traffic isn't bad at 6:00 P.M. If the person was really intent on accomplishing an objective, he would have left early to compensate for bad traffic. Are you a **make-it-happen** type? We want to give you tough objectives and say, "Bill will get it done. Mary will get it done. Just give it to them. They will bring it back to you successfully completed."

There are a few points that I have recommended you write on your shirt cuff, the back of your hand, or certainly on a 3 X 5 card. One of the major points to write down is, "Have I projected to the recruiter I am a **make-it-happen**, goal-/mission-oriented, success-driven person?"

Enthusiasm

In addition to the basics of intellect and communication skills, recruiters look for enthusiasm. We love to see individuals who are excited to get out of bed in the morning — excited about doing whatever they have to do. It doesn't make any difference whether we're picking somebody to play bridge, throw horseshoes, play basketball, or hire as an employee. We like people who have a sparkle in their eye and a smile on their face. They can laugh at themselves. They create a positive, pleasant, professional aura about themselves.

I have seen people with enthusiasm have great success at interviewing. Other people with even better credentials have not done as well because they simply didn't have that sparkle in their eye. I've seen enthusiasm outweigh some negatives in the interview. Recruiters say, "Roger, there are some things I don't like about this applicant, but I have to tell you something. She is so enthusiastic and upbeat, and is someone I would want to work for us. I have absolutely no doubt we can work through a couple of the things in her background that could have been better." When you go on an interview, don't leave the enthusiasm at home whether the interview is with Roger Cameron or a major corporate recruiter. We're all the same. We love to see enthusiastic individuals. There is no factor that assures that enthusiasm in itself will get you a job, but it irons out a lot of wrinkles in an applicant's background. And, smile — a smile attracts a smile. Try it today. Try it in an interview.

Putting Success Into Words

What you've done in the past is an indication of what you'll do in the future. However, I find so many officers who simply expect us to look at their evaluations or resumes and see that they've been successful in the past. If that were the case, a company would simply tell you, "Send us your resume." They would take a look at it, and then mail you a job offer. Please understand. You must be able to communicate past successes. The key word is **communicate**.

One of the most frequent questions asked in an interview is this: "Give me an example of a significant accomplishment. **Why** was it significant and **how** did you accomplish it?" You must **verbalize** your past successes. There is probably no other question on which you need to spend as much time. You must prepare one to three examples of successful achievements in high school, college, and the military.

Remember: **Listen carefully**. Was the question, "Give me **a** significant accomplishment," or "Give me your **most** significant accomplishment," or "Give me an accomplishment in your **first job** in the military?"

Consider your **most** significant accomplishment in your recent experience in the military. As you gain age and maturity, and achieve rank and higher compensation, you can be expected to have more significant objectives, and, therefore, greater accomplishments.

Imagine this: After five years in the military, you are sitting in front of a company recruiter. You're a captain — but you're saying your greatest accomplishment happened during the time you were a second lieutenant. That really doesn't make much sense.

"That's A Good Question"
The recruiter does not need to be told that he/she has asked a good question. Unless you do it every time, the recruiter may assume that the other questions are not good ones. Why do people say this? They buy time while they're thinking about

the answer. It is not necessary for you to say anything. Just take three to six seconds to reflect and then respond.

"How Did I Do?"

This is a very poor question. A recruiter's job is not to give you instant feedback on whether your interview was good, bad, or indifferent. We want you to know yourself. We want you to have the confidence that you have answered the questions with substance and depth, so you know as you leave it was a good interview. Do **not** ask the recruiter, "How did I do?"

Making Eye Contact

It's critical that, as you give an answer to a recruiter, you have solid eye contact with that recruiter. Have confidence in your answers. Show that confidence by looking the recruiter directly in the eye.

Often, applicants tend to lose eye contact when it's most important — with a difficult question that may be uncomfortable to answer. That's when I see eyes go to the floor, the ceiling, the window. You simply cannot do this.

Have you noticed that people "talk" with their eyes? Eyes can sparkle, look bland, or look suspicious. Don't you find you often make judgments based upon what you see in someone's eyes? Don't you question when someone doesn't look **you** in the eye? You may think, "Are they interested, bored, uncaring, or lacking self-confidence?" Eyes should show enthusiasm, understanding, curiosity, warmth, and feeling.

Be aware of your eye contact. Where do you look when you talk to someone? Do you look at their mouth or do you look them in the eye? If you are not accustomed to having direct eye contact, it can be awkward at first, but if you concentrate and practice, you will become comfortable with it. Eye contact should be natural, so do not "stare people down." Glance away about 10% of the time.

With good eye contact, **you will appear more confident and self-assured. People will listen to you and actually hear more of what you say.** Almost all of us can improve our eye contact, so make yourself conscious of yours and work to make it better.

Two Or More Recruiters
Frequently, two recruiters will interview you at the same time. Determine if both recruiters will be in the interview. If one recruiter is placed out of your normal eyesight, don't include him in the interview. Simply greet him at the beginning of the interview and afterwards. Be sure to remember both recruiters' names.

If you are interviewed by two recruiters, you need to maintain eye contact with both when you answer a question. However, you need to give the one who asks the question the initial and concluding eye contact. In other words, let's say Recruiter A asks you a question. Begin your answer with eye contact with Recruiter A. Continue your answer and pick up eye contact with Recruiter B. Conclude your answer with eye contact with Recruiter A. If the question is substantive and requires a lengthy answer, you may change eye contact several times, always ending by getting eye contact with the recruiter who asked the question.

Never be worried about an interview with two or more recruiters. I almost prefer it. Usually, they ask questions at the same time and that allows the choice of which question to answer. Talk to them as you would with friends in your living room.

Always remember, companies are looking for young men and women who have poise and self-confidence. These qualities are important in group meetings as well as one-on-one situations.

Closing The Interview
When is an interview over? The most common signal that the interview is nearing its end is when the recruiter looks at you and asks if you have any questions. Before you answer, keep two crucial considerations in mind. First, did you give poor answers to any questions during the interview that might cause the recruiter to **rule you out**? If you've given a poor answer to a question, but the recruiter has given you very positive indications that he or she is going to invite you back for another follow-up interview, or give you an offer, be quiet. Don't go back and bring up a negative.

Secondly, what strong positive factors in your background were not brought out by the recruiter's questions? You might want to go back and say, "I do have some questions; however, before I ask them, I feel there are some things I need to tell you about myself that weren't brought out in the interview." Do it **only** if you feel that it can have some **positive influence** on the outcome of the interview. If you already have those positive signals, then get out of the interview as quickly as possible once you've asked your questions. I've seen applicants lose interviews they had won because they stayed in the room and brought up irrelevant information or reminded a recruiter of a negative that came up during the course of the interview. **Be smart**.

If you've given answers you feel are not satisfactory, do you remember what the question was? Go back and restate your attitude and your answer. Do it better. End on a positive note, not a negative one.

If you've missed an opportunity to give information that's important to your job pursuit, then do so at the conclusion. For example, you might say, "I've had a position similar to this one," giving details.

**DON'T USE MY WORDS.
USE MY THOUGHTS.**

Now, we come to the questions you may have. Show your intellectual curiosity by asking **high-quality** questions. Major corporate recruiters look for individuals who are "growable" — people who are constantly working to improve their base of knowledge in relation to their career. These people have a high degree of curiosity, and this shows in their questions.

I recall being at a business conference with many successful people from around the country. At the start, we were asked to introduce ourselves, tell where we were from, what our careers were about — and also to name three people we would like to have as dinner guests.

Many people said the President of the United States, a famous public figure, an actor, a politician, etc. But, as I listened to everyone, I thought: Is that what would really be important to me?

I was the last to get up. I told the group that the three people with whom I'd most like to have dinner would be people who were **full of curiosity.** I didn't care if they were plumbers or carpenters or housekeepers. It made no difference. I knew I'd enjoy an extremely interesting dinner if I were simply with people who exhibited a high degree of curiosity.

Curious people ask questions. They are interested in what's happening. We want people who are curious. When you ask questions, you get answers. When you get answers, you become more knowledgeable. You are what we call a **growable** person.

Make sure you have an accurate perception of the industry involved, the company, the position open, the people interviewing you, and what you want to do in your career.

Close the interview by being **upbeat**. Applicants sometimes walk away from interviews in which they have a high degree of interest without pressing that interest with a high degree of enthusiasm. If you are truly interested in the company and in the position, you cannot afford to leave the interview without letting the recruiter know that. Do not tell the recruiter you have a strong interest if you do not. There are going to be times when you interview with a high quality company which, for one reason or another, just does not fit with your career goals at the time. You should not mislead the recruiter by overstating your interest.

Let me say again that, if you have an interest in the company, you cannot afford to walk out of the interview without showing a high degree of interest. You must make your close **personal** and **specific**. Make a statement that could **only** be relevant to this company. For instance, "I have a strong interest in Quaker Oats. I was impressed by many things, but most of all by the statements your president and CEO, Mr. William D. Smithburg, made in your 1991 annual report beginning on page 2. I'm impressed with your sole concentration on grocery products and your concept of 'controllable earnings.' I look forward to having another interview with your company or to receiving an offer from your company" (depending on where you are in the interviewing procedure). This response needs to be **sincere** and **upbeat**. Notice this statement could not be made about another company. Someone else wouldn't even know what you were talking about. This is the true test of a good close. You may not have a lot of time for a close, yet you **must** deliver it. Have your points well-ingrained in your mind for fluid and believable delivery.

Sometimes, an applicant just doesn't know **when** to get out of an interview. If you have a positive response and the interviewer says, "I'm very excited about what I see. We'd like to invite you for a follow-up interview," then, it's time to get up and leave. The purpose of the interview has been accomplished by both parties.

DON'T USE MY WORDS.
USE MY THOUGHTS.

Sending Thank-You Notes

Following your initial interview, be sure to write thank-you notes to those companies that have expressed an interest in pursuing you further. The purpose of sending such a note is to restate your strong interest in the company and your desire for a follow-up interview. To help you with this task, here are some guidelines.

1) Using quality plain paper, you can either write or type your notes. If your handwriting or printing is not neat, you should type your letters on a good computer or typewriter. Pay close attention to your spelling, sentence structure,

grammar, and punctuation. Mistakes in these areas will ruin the message you are trying to convey.

2) **Never** ask a question in your letter that forces a recruiter to respond to your letter. You want to motivate them to take action and make arrangements for the next step, not increase their paperwork.

3) Write your letters immediately, and send them no later than the weekend after the interview. Other applicants will be sending their thank-you notes promptly, and if yours is delayed, the company could assume a lack of interest on your part.

4) **Do** tell a company when you have chosen them as one of your top companies. Remember how good you feel when you know someone thinks highly of you.

5) Do not start your letter thanking a company for taking the time to interview you. Instead, focus on how much you enjoyed the time spent with the recruiter learning more about the company and the positions discussed.

6) Tailor each letter to each individual company. A form letter will do you more harm than good. A personalized letter expresses the **sincere** interest you have in a particular company. Take a few moments to reflect on the interview and determine why you are excited about that company. Then, create a letter which will communicate your desire for follow-up interviews and inspire the recruiter to pursue you further.

7) If, because of your availability or other reasons, a company has not started pursuit within 30 days of the initial interview,

you should send another note. Again, you should reiterate your interest and confirm your date of availability.

8) I want to caution you. Please realize the massive amount of mail that any corporate recruiter or department manager gets in a day. Why not try to be unique in sending a piece of mail? What's wrong with sending an envelope that is a different color? I just wonder — if I got 20 pieces of mail in the morning, 19 of them are white and one of them is red — wouldn't the red one catch my eye? Have you ever received a telegram and not opened it immediately? Did you ever receive an overnight letter and not immediately want to know what it was and open it? I remember one time that I opened the mail and out rolled what looked like a stick of dynamite. It actually was a paper tube with a fuse sticking out of the top. Ingenious. Unique. And you can bet it was absolutely the first piece of mail I picked up and opened. Please don't be afraid to be professionally unique. Corporate America likes people who are innovative and creative. Dare to be innovative and unique from a marketing standpoint. Good luck!

9) If you're working with a **quality recruiting firm** which conveys a company's interest to you and your interest to the company, you should not send a thank-you letter since your recruiting firm is doing that for you. Always remember, the point is to let the company know you have interest, not to inundate them with irrelevant letters. If the recruiting firm is not helping you with follow-up or communication with the company, then you must write these letters yourself.

Follow-up Interviews

I have observed applicants work very hard and become very competitive in their initial interviews. They are invited for follow-up interviews and think they're over the hump and on the downhill side. You are **never** on the downhill side until you have an offer. We've seen too many times in football games where a team gets out in front. It appears obvious to them they will win. They let up. The next thing you know, they are defeated. You, undoubtedly, have had this happen to you sometime in your own life. You knew you were in a winning situation. All of a sudden, you found yourself defeated. **When you prepare yourself for a follow-up interview, prepare even harder than you did for your initial interviews.**

I have been excited about applicants I've accepted and looked forward to introducing them to some of my client companies. Three months later, I would go to their particular base to better prepare them for interviewing, but this time, they just wouldn't impress me. Why? They knew they had been accepted. They assumed once they were accepted, they could never be declined — which is certainly not true. You can never let up. You can never feel you are home safe until the offer to go to work for a company is in your pocket.

Once a recruiter has said "yes" to a preliminary interview, normally you'll go through a series of follow-up interviews. You could receive as little as 24 hours notice of an interview trip, and you need to be ready. Get your suits and your "professional casual" travel clothes cleaned and pressed, shine your shoes, and ensure your travel essentials are easily accessible. Also, organize your corporate information, and keep it handy.

Here are some broad guidelines to follow when a company calls you:

Broad Guidelines For Follow-Up Interview Calls
- **Take notes**. Write down **everything**. Take the name,

number, and title/job of the person calling if you don't know him/her. Write down any specific information that is given. Ideally, take notes on or in your calendar or datebook.

- **Don't assume.** Applicants have been brought in for jobs or locations that were different from those discussed. Company representatives (particularly if they are human resources/recruiting assistants) may not have complete information about you, and they may assume, for example, that you know they are in a certain location when you really do not know their location.

- **Ask questions.** Verify what you "think." The person with whom you are speaking may "only want answers to two quick questions," yet may have all kinds of information that would be helpful to you.

- **Close the call.** At the end of the call, confirm you have correctly recorded all the details and verify what (if anything) you will have to do next: make reservations, call the company back after checking on something, etc. Also, find out what **the company** will be doing to set up your logistics.

- **Be your smart self.** The person calling could be your future boss! Show energy, enthusiasm, and appreciation for his/her continued interest. Don't burn your bridges.

After being notified of an upcoming interview, you must increase your level of knowledge of the industry, company, and position for which you are interviewing. Quality companies have come to consider a lack of such effort to be indicative of either a lack of interest or a lack of follow-through, both of which are **dangerous**. You should read any books you have not yet finished and also find the best library to do general industry reading and company research.

If you know the location for which you are being considered, call the local Chamber of Commerce and have them send you information. Look up specifics in the library, too. Below are some industries that lend themselves easily to research you can do right away:

- **Medical instrument companies** — Go to hospitals and speak with doctors, surgeons, and purchasing agents. (Wear a suit for these meetings.) Tell them that you are interviewing for a position with Company XYZ. Ask what they like and don't like about the company product. Is the price competitive? Is the quality consistent? Are they pleased with the sales representative? What is the competition doing better or worse?

- **Pharmaceutical companies** — Visit pharmacies and doctors. If you are interviewing for a sales position, go to non-chain drugstores where the pharmacist will have purchasing decisions. As with the medical companies, ask questions to understand the company's reputation and the quality of their product.

- **Consumer products** — Visit grocery stores and try to speak with the manager and ask about the company's product and the competition. Where is the product located on the shelf? How is it priced? What colors and print do they use in the packaging? Ask customers you see at the store why they chose or did not choose the product. Check out the Sunday paper for coupons. What do you notice about the color, expiration date, and discount amount? Watch for all advertisements in the media. See if you can speak with the local sales representative.

- **Retail stores or distribution centers** — Visit local stores, if possible. Try to speak with the manager. How is the store laid out? Do you feel welcome? How are the items merchandised? Is the store light and bright? How are the prices? Ask questions about the transportation department. How often is merchandise delivered? What are the top selling items?

- **Quick service restaurants** — Do some market research. Visit the local restaurants and their competition. Analyze the prices, the menu selection, and the variety. How happy are the employees? How clean is the restaurant? How long are you kept waiting? How is the restaurant being advertised? What are the coupons, commercials, and signs on the windows like? Where is the location? Is it a drive-in, eat-in, or take-out restaurant only? What works? What would you want to change?

Once you have been invited on a follow-up interview, the first thing you need to do is ensure that you have all your travel logistics completely arranged and that you understand how you will be getting from place to place. If you will be traveling by air, the company may send your tickets in the mail or, depending on any timing constraints, perhaps by an overnight mail service. If you are flying with an airline and are a member of that airline's frequent flyer program, be sure to get proper credit for your flight. If you don't belong, be sure to sign up before the flight! If the tickets will be pre-paid at the airport, you **must** be at the airport at least one hour prior to departure with two types of picture identification. Some companies will ask you to purchase your own tickets and will reimburse you. In this case, you will usually complete an expense report and will be reimbursed before you receive the bill from your credit card company.

Remember that airline tickets are the same as money. You should never discard unused portions of your ticket, and you should keep the copies for receipts. If a company asks you to make your own airline reservations, do not book reservations with penalties which restrict changes. On occasion, it will be necessary or preferred to arrange the follow-up interviews of two separate companies on back-to-back days, possibly combining the travel plans. It is very important that you take extreme care to divide costs fairly between the companies involved. You should **never** see one company on another company's money.

If you will be traveling by car, make sure you have precise directions to prevent you from getting lost and being late. **Always** try to arrive at your destination no later than 6:00 P.M. to ensure getting in early enough to relax and benefit from a full night's sleep.

Now that you have all of your travel arrangements confirmed, you need to verify that every step in the process is covered. "Every step" means your transportation from

1) **Your home to airport.** You may be driving yourself to the airport in your own car, or perhaps your spouse or a friend will drop you off. Whatever your means of transportation, plan ahead so that you make it to the airport **at least** one hour prior to your flight departure time. Don't let yourself get into a "traffic jam." If you do, you will be rushing to make your flight, and you will be nervous before you even start your journey. I have seen applicants miss their flights due to poor planning, which showed nothing to the company but that they lacked good judgment. Plan ahead for traffic congestion, gas purchases, a full parking lot, or any other "problem" that might come up that would delay

or prevent you from arriving at your flight on time to board the plane.

2) **Airport to airport.** If you are going to have a layover, determine how much time you have between flights. If your first flight had any delays, will that cause you to miss your next flight, and if so, what will your strategy be then? For example, let's say you know you have a 45-minute layover in the Atlanta airport. When you arrive at your boarding gate at the point of origin, ask the attendant for the gate number at which you will be arriving in Atlanta, and the gate number from which you will be departing. By doing this, you will know if a short walk or a fast run is required to reach your next plane. If there will be a distance between gates, ask someone if a shuttle bus is available and if it can speed up your time. Always carry all necessary phone numbers with you in case a situation develops that may cause a delay while you are in transit.

Also, before you leave on your trip, get the phone number of the hotel at which you are staying. You never know what might occur while you are traveling. If your connecting flight is canceled or if you have any other difficulties during travel, you should leave a message at the hotel's front desk explaining your situation to whoever will be meeting you. As a basic rule, hotel rooms are held until 6:00 P.M. for the arriving guest. To guarantee your room for a late arrival, you will need to give a credit card number to the reservation desk. Therefore, when you get details for your hotel, be sure to get the confirmation number and verify that the room will be held for late arrival. If you will be unable to arrive as planned due to a canceled flight, you **must** call the hotel prior to 6:00 P.M. and get a cancellation number. Otherwise, your credit card will be charged!

3) **Airport to hotel.** When you confirm your travel arrangements, be sure to find out who will be picking you up at the airport. Will it be a taxi? A limo service? Will there be a company representative there for you? If so, what should you wear? And, where will you be met? At the gate? Baggage claim? The curb outside Terminal 1? Will you know what the persons meeting you look like and what they will be wearing? Or, will they be holding a sign that has your name on it?

You may be picking up a rental car at the aiport. If so, you must have a valid credit card issued with your name on it and available credit. You must also have a current driver's license. Be aware that car rental companies have rules that restrict them from renting to individuals unless they meet certain age qualifications. Check with some of the major rental companies to determine current regulations. If you do rent a car, determine how you will get to the hotel from the airport. You must have detailed instructions in hand prior to getting in that car so that you know where you are going. Always carry the phone number of the hotel at which you will be staying. Your hotel reservations will usually be made by the company, but, occasionally, alternative directions will be given to you. Your hotel costs may be billed directly to the company, or the company may ask you to pay and will reimburse you. Again, you will usually complete an expense report.

4) **Hotel to company.** Determine if a company representative will pick you up and, if so, what time. If you must drive to the company, do you have accurate directions? How long will it take to get there? Should you do a test run to make sure there are no detours or other obstacles? Where will you meet the company representative? In the lobby of the hotel? Outside? Who will it be? Have you met them before?

Even if this individual may not participate in your actual "interview," he or she will still be evaluating you and forming an opinion of you.

Do not leave one step out. Make sure you can address each step so you don't get to the airport in the middle of the night and suddenly realize nobody told you how you were supposed to get to the hotel. If you are given an itinerary over the phone, go over it mentally **before** you hang up. Also, take at least $100 cash with you, and keep all your receipts so you can get fully reimbursed. **Carry on your luggage.** You **don't** want to arrive without your interview suit and toiletries. It has happened before. **Don't let it happen to you!**

Items to bring to your follow-up interview:
1) Your resume.
2) Company literature.
3) *PCS To Corporate America.*
4) Three personal and three professional references, including names, titles, addresses, and phone numbers.

Start final preparation for your follow-up interview no later than one night before the interview is to take place. Then, on your flight, you can review all of the material one more time so that you will thoroughly understand the information. Review all of the information listed above to maximize your chances for success.

You may think you are an interviewing expert now. You are not because you have only become good at initial interviews, not follow-ups. While you should be quite confident, there are some areas to which you have not been exposed that could occur.

Most companies today, when hiring a development candidate, will want a unanimous decision — having all managers say "thumbs up" to an applicant. It is not good to have even one manager say "no" to you when, in fact, you might one day work for that individual. It doesn't create the best working environment. Most companies require a unanimous decision by all managers. This means every person with whom you interview is an important person in getting an offer from that company. Therefore, make each person feel he or she is important to the decision. You must go to every interview armed with questions for that interviewer. You cannot ask a question and show no interest in the answer. You should never ask a question when you already know the answer. That means when you get ready to go on a follow-up, you need to have many questions at your disposal. This is one of the most important moves you're going to make in your career.

Wrap up every interview in a positive manner. During the follow-up interview, **tell the recruiter you want an offer**. I don't care what the words are. I don't care how you do it. I've had applicants come back and say, "Roger, I couldn't because we ran out of time" — or some other such excuse. When I find that they didn't close the interview, I say, "Look, there's no reason for me to explain how to do something if you're not going to listen." The applicants say to me, "Roger, you know the interview went up to the last second, and I didn't have time to close the interview in an upbeat manner." I always look at that applicant and say, "I don't want to hear about it. I don't care if you have to throw your body at the foot of the door before you leave somebody's office. **You must close that interview**."

Please recall, as reviewed on page 129, your close must be company specific. It must also be delivered with sincerity. Or, again, if it is the company you want to go to work for and you already know that, let the recruiter know it. "This is my choice — the company I want to work for. I want you to know I'm looking forward to receiving an offer from your company and accepting it." I don't care how you do it. **You must do it before you leave the interview.** That recruiter may be interviewing three or four different people. If three of them have stated an interest and one doesn't, you can bet the one who doesn't is **not** going to pull the offer. Exceptions are rare. You wouldn't want to roll the dice for the exception.

Once again, I want to remind you of professionalism. If you cannot see yourself working in this company or if the position is not right for you, stop. Don't mislead the company or the recruiters. Thank them for the follow-up interview. Tell them you appreciate the opportunity to get a better look at what the position and the company is all about, but it is not right for you. Don't have them make the offer to you and turn down other applicants who have a very strong interest in the position. If you're not sure this is the company you want to work for, be careful what you tell them. You must later be able to live with the comments you make. Be professional. Corporate America is a small world. You want to be proud of your ethics and professionalism should you ever run into employees of the company or the recruiter later. **Never burn a bridge.**

If the follow-up interview happens to put you out on the manufacturing floor, you must get involved. Many times, you feel as if you're simply getting an opportunity to see the manufacturing plant. But, recruiters are going to look for a high degree of interest and curiosity from you. Don't be afraid to ask permission to cross safety lines to take a closer look at a piece of equipment. Don't walk through a plant and not have numerous questions about what you have seen. One of the most fascinating experiences in the world is to go through a major manufacturing facility. I'm not an engineer, but I'm always overwhelmed by what great engineers have done in different manufacturing processes. I could go through a manufacturing plant, and it would take me a week to get all my questions answered. It's that exciting. You must show that excitement.

I have seen an applicant go through a plant and have the person who was taking him on the tour introduce him to a laborer on the floor. The tour guide then said, "Excuse me a minute; I see someone over here I need to speak with. I'll be right back." The company was one that emphasized participative management, and they watched the applicant to see if he developed a conversation with that worker. If you find yourself in a similar situation, develop a conversation and remember the individual's name.

Imagine being taken into offices of manufacturing facilities to be interviewed. You can't know that the recruiter has taken the name plaque off his desk as well as memorabilia or plaques hanging on his wall that include his name. He introduces himself to you when you come in. As you're walking out the door, he shakes your hand, looks you in the eye and says, "What is my name?" Please (in a participative management world) don't forget his name. If you use your spiral notebook as I've suggested, this won't happen to you. Also, it would have been embarrassing for you not to have been using his name two or three times during the course of the interview.

If you are interviewing for a sales position, as a part of the follow-up process, you will probably be invited to spend a day in the field with a local sales representative. Remember, this person is doing you a favor by taking extra time from a busy schedule to show you the job. Be extremely polite and considerate. Arrive at the agreed-upon destination 15 minutes early. Come dressed in your best interviewing suit, unless other attire is specifically requested. (Special Note: If you are going into a hospital where you may tour surgery areas, ask if you will need tennis shoes.) If you meet for a meal, there is no need to offer to pay, as the sales representative will put it on an expense report. However, it is important to thank your host. **You must get involved. This is not a time for you to simply follow along behind and not interact. Remember, you are being evaluated.** Do whatever you can to help out and make the sales representative's day easier. Offer to carry a briefcase, park the car, or anything else you think would be helpful. Make **elaborate** notes of each account on which you call. Who was called on? For what purpose? Write down questions you have of the sales technique used or questions asked and responses. Do not do anything to interfere negatively with the sales calls. Your social skills will be observed and noted. Be polite and friendly but not obtrusive. When you are back in the car driving to the next sales call, then is the time to demonstrate your curiosity and insight by asking good questions. At the end of the day, remember to ask for the sales representative's card. Then, call and/or write to express thanks again for the valuable time that was spent with you. It is up to you to make that individual comfortable about referring you on to the next step.

I have watched applicants spend a day in the field with a sales representative. Never once did they offer to help carry the briefcase of the salesperson. They never showed curiosity and did not even take notes. They forgot the clients they met. You must be involved. You're not out there simply for the sake of observation. You're there for the company to see what your interest is in the position. Be able to show your intelligence and how you perceive the position, the industry, and the company through the questions you ask.

It's a shame to go through all the work and preparation — buying the right suits, building the right resume, getting through the initial interview, learning how to answer the important questions — and then fail in the final interview by not staying constantly alert and thoroughly involved. The minute you're on company money, you had better be focused totally on that company. The minute you walk out of the door at home, the company is paying every penny of your expenses. Therefore, it is only appropriate for you to give them every ounce of your concentration.

Eating

Using good manners and good judgment while you eat is also an important factor in the interviewing environment. I've seen too many applicants lose an offer because of what they did at dinner. Always finish your meal. Not eating suggests you are too nervous and lack poise and self-confidence.

The company will be paying, so be aware of the cost of what you order. Don't select the most expensive entree on the menu. That suggests that you don't understand expenses. Today, companies can't always write off all meal expenses.

When you order, be aware that foods with sauces can be difficult to eat without spotting your clothes. The primary purpose of the meal is to interview rather than eat. Therefore, order foods that are easy to handle — thereby reducing the risk of unsightly stains.

You may think it won't happen to you, but I've seen it happen to the very best applicants. It's very embarrassing to have a spot on your tie, shirt or pants, blouse or skirt, for the balance of an interview — especially if the spilling happened at breakfast. Getting yourself into that kind of situation suggests you aren't controlling your environment. You're losing sight of the meal's objective — which is to provide an opportunity to interview.

For dinner, I suggest ordering a sautéed fish entree. Fish is easy to get into the mouth and dissolves quickly. I've watched applicants tackle entrees they must chew repeatedly. A lot of chewing doesn't allow you the crucial time to answer and ask questions.

Also, remember your manners. Since we live in such a fast-paced world, rules of etiquette are often never learned — or, at best, forgotten. However, business is often conducted over meals and having good manners is very important to you. Here are some of the major tips:

- Don't start eating before your host or hostess begins.
- Cut your food up as you eat it — not all at once.
- Use your napkin.
- Don't eat while you are talking.
- Chew with your mouth closed.
- Place the napkin on your lap with the crease toward you. Never tuck it in your belt or collar.
- Remember the rule of thumb: "Solids on the left; liquids on the right." This may help you avoid using someone else's water glass instead of your own.
- Don't serve yourself items such as salt, pepper, sugar, and salad dressing before you offer it to someone else.
- Don't salt your food before you taste it. It could be a signal that you are a person who makes rash decisions.
- Spoon soup away from you and sip it from the side of the spoon — without slurping.
- Remove olive pits, bones, etc., from your mouth discreetly with a fork.

Drinking
I feel there is absolutely no excuse for drinking alcohol during an interview — period. If offered a drink, you may say, "I do drink on occasion, but not while I'm interviewing." If the

recruiter doesn't accept that as professional behavior, you probably wouldn't want to work for that company anyway.

Again, there can be no reason for drinking alcohol in an interview, and as far as I'm concerned, the recruiter shouldn't be drinking either.

See Appendix D for a self-evaluation sheet to use after each interview.

Facing The Big Questions

"PCS to Corporate America is to a junior military officer what a playbook is to the professional quarterback. Roger has transferred years of experience and knowledge into the most comprehensive guidebook to assist the JMO in the transition from the military to Corporate America. This book was an invaluable resource during my transition to a civilian career. Roger Cameron is without a doubt the recruiting 'guru' and the primary reason for my company's exclusive choice of Cameron-Brooks as a recruiter."

— Paul Kapsner
Regional Sales Manager
Snowden-Pencer, Inc.

CHAPTER 6

Facing The Big Questions — Developing The Best Answers

Probably the best learning experience an applicant could have would be to sit in the corner of my hotel room and listen to other applicants interviewing. I have brought members of my staff to military bases to sit in the room and watch and listen as I conduct interviews throughout the course of the day. They will each tell you they were amazed at what they saw applicants do and not do and their demeanor throughout the course of an interview.

Many applicants come before recruiters as if they're carrying the weight of the world on their shoulders. We want someone to be relaxed, not afraid to smile, and eager to be there. Make the conversation flow. Too often, we find the military officer to be very stiff. While we certainly understand you have some butterflies in your stomach, attempt to show a lighter, more at ease, professional style.

It's crucial to understand the two basic philosophies which are the foundation blocks for probably 90% of the questions you will be asked. The number one block is the understanding of how one judges success — by the accomplishment of objective. From the derelict on the park bench to the president of the United States, every one of us is identical in the way we judge success. What makes us uniquely different as individuals are our objectives. The derelict's objectives are different from ours, but we judge success in precisely the same way.

How do you judge the **quality** of a success? Obviously, not every success can be of equal quality. Consequently, we judge the quality of success by the **difficulty** factor. The greater the degree of **difficulty**, the greater the significance of the accomplishment. You must realize that if success is the accomplishment of an objective, the flip side of the coin is that failure must simply be the nonaccomplishment of an objective. You can have a slight failure or a catastrophic failure. You can have a slight success, or you can have a phenomenal success. Remember, in giving your answers, don't state the degree of success. Verbalize the success in such a way that the recruiter can determine the degree of success or the degree of failure.

The second fundamental philosophy applicants must have is that of being individuals who can grow and progress — not people who think they have already maxed out their ability to improve at age 27 or 28. Many questions will address your attitude about taking constructive comments from management. Some people are difficult to manage. *FORTUNE 500* companies do not need to hire management problems. We want people who are team players and respond well to management's directives.

Frequently, a question is asked, "If you take all of the assets you have and use on a daily basis, which ones do you feel you **can** improve upon?" Obviously, the key word is **can**. The attitude we're looking for in applicants is that they can improve upon everything they're doing and would hope to be able to do so even at age 98. You can give an excellent speech, but you can give an even better speech. You can have a great command, but you can have an even better command. You can run a four-minute mile, but you can run an even faster mile. We look for people with great attitudes about expanding themselves.

The question, "Which one of your assets do you feel that you **need** to improve?" can give you some difficulty. **Need,** by definition, means that you have a significant weakness in that area. I can't imagine Procter & Gamble, Mobil Oil, or any other great company coming to me and saying, "Roger, travel around the world and let us pay you $8,000 to $10,000 to hire an individual who has weaknesses." Be careful to distinguish between the word **can** and **need.** You must always be honest. If you have deficiencies, you need to be willing and able to talk about those deficiencies. Refer to "Covering Your Weaknesses" on page 66. Hopefully, you're doing something about them. You can point out a program you are in at that very moment which is helping you bring the deficiency up to a strength. Know yourself. Know your strengths and your weaknesses. Feel comfortable in being able to talk about them knowing when you put the strengths on the scale, they will far outweigh any weaknesses you might have.

You Must Interview In The First Person
I don't think there's anything worse than the officer who talks in the second person. Don't use the word "you." **I'm** not the one being evaluated in the interview — **you** are.

Sometimes, an applicant says, "I feel that's what a person should do." I beg your pardon! We're not hiring a third party — we're hiring **you.** You must talk in the **first** person.

It's absolutely amazing how hard we have to work with applicants to get them to interview in the first person.

You're going into an interview to be evaluated for **your** abilities to accomplish difficult objectives — and motivate people. **You** must tell us that in the first person, and there can be no exception.

Remember, we're not having a philosophical conversation. If we were, we could use the second person. In an interview, the entire objective is to determine whether or not to offer **you** a job. The first person usage is critical to **your** success.

Listen to others around you talk — notice how often they slide into the second person. In some branches of the military, they teach you to talk and write this way. But, as you're interviewing with Corporate America, you must know how we talk. Listen carefully to the examples you put on your tape recorder. If you are excessive in the use of the second person, it will be a factor to rule you out.

In interviews, you must individualize your accomplishments. We expect to hear you say "I." Otherwise, we would have no ability to know what you accomplish versus what someone else accomplishes. **Be careful in wording your accomplishments. You must demonstrate the ability to be an individual, and yet be a team player.** I know of no company in America that will hire an individual who is not a team player. We want a person who can interact with others, whether they are subordinates, peers, or superiors. So, be careful. In today's participative world, you must come across strongly as a team player.

Projecting Yourself As A Team Player
As Corporate America becomes more participative in its leadership style, as we de-emphasize titles, and as we look harder for those who can lead without being "the boss," we want people who can be team players. Simply stated, team players are individuals who have as much concern for their fellow workers and department's or company's success as for their own.

Being a team player is easier said than done. Some people find it impossible. While moving up the corporate ladder will always be important to you, a value for individual competitiveness should be subtle at best. Corporate America expects a philosophy that emphasizes helping others to be successful and accomplish their corporate and personal goals.

I encourage you to examine your philosophy and determine whether you are known as a team player who works for the good of the team or as an individual who is more concerned about number one. If it's the latter, I recommend you take immediate steps to rethink the importance of being a team player.

"Tell Me About Yourself"

The recruiter says to you, **"Tell me about yourself."** There will hardly ever be an interview where that question is not asked. Too many applicants feel that this is a license to bore the recruiter. I have had applicants take up the entire 30-minute interview telling me about themselves, but not covering the issues in which I had any interest. Some interviewing books encourage you to take 20 to 40 minutes for your answer. I disagree. I feel you should talk no more than two to three minutes on high school, the same on college, and the same on the military. In your answers, there are only two things that you should cover — your goals and your accomplishments. Note: no rhetoric, just goals and accomplishments.

When interviewers ask this question, they are attempting to determine if you are at the "helm" of your vehicle (your personal life). They want to be assured you're solidly in the front seat, behind the steering wheel making sure you're "driving" your life in the direction you want it to go. Too many people appear to ride on the passenger side and, sadly, some seem to be riding in the trunk. There are only **three** words that can give the proper perspective to a recruiter — **want, goal,** or **objective.** These three words closely state you are in control of your life and are working to make your life successful. We recognize that you'll expect to be put in charge of a unit, department, or division of the company you join, and we want to feel confident you'll, by nature, step to the "helm" of that unit.

I'll give you an example of an individual who had no understanding of the need to direct his life by first discovering his own wants and goals and then acting upon them decisively. A short time ago, I interviewed a young development candidate. His spouse was also present during the interview. About 20 minutes into the interview, I sensed his spouse becoming "uptight." She crossed her arms, leaned back in the chair, and arched her back — all signs of tensing up. I wasn't quite sure what was causing it, even though I hoped I wasn't giving her any cause to be upset. Suddenly, she interrupted the interview in an explosive manner, looked at her husband, and in a fierce voice, asked him if he had ever made a decision on his own! Then she said, "I can tell you, I wouldn't hire you!"

I admit I was uncomfortable observing this scenario, but not as uncomfortable as I would have been if I had been riding down in the elevator with them after I proceeded to rule her husband out.

Let's take a look at the interview. I was using the "Why" interview as described in a subsequent topic. I asked the applicant why he chose his college. He told me that he had never planned to go to college, but two of his best friends talked him into going and so he went where they went. I asked why he selected biology as his major. He really didn't know what he wanted to do, but because he had a good friend whom he respected who chose biology, he thought it would be good for him also. I then asked why he joined a fraternity and again it was because of a friend. This applicant's direction in school and in life reflected no goal or objective. He was not at the "helm" of his life — it was being steered by someone else.

Here is an example of an appropriate reply given by an individual who was asked to tell about himself: "I'm an only child of a Texas farm family. When I went to high school, there were several things I **wanted to** accomplish. First of all, I wanted a grade point average (goal) that would allow me to get into the college of my choice. I was accepted by Texas A & M (accomplishment). I also knew that I wanted to play sports (goal). I was a wrestler and a football player (accomplishment)." Remember, we're taking a hard look to see if you are goal-oriented and have the ability to **make it happen!** Notice I didn't say goal, accomplishment, **detail.** At this point, you will not be going into detail as to why you set the goal or how you accomplished it.

As you discuss a point of interest, recruiters may interrupt to ask questions. They will want to know why that goal was important to you and how you accomplished it. Be sensitive to the recruiters and allow them to enter in. This approach allows the recruiters to ask you to elaborate on a point of interest that is important.

When you are interrupted, it's critical that you remember exactly where you were when interrupted, so when you finish answering the recruiter's question, you can come back smoothly, picking up where you left off. You **should never** look at the recruiter after elaborating on a point and say, "Now where was I?" After all, it is your story.

Why Are You Leaving The Military?
Unfortunately, many officers feel they must knock the military.

They think they have to be negative in order to explain why they're leaving. **DON'T.**

It's our position that if you're negative about Company A (the military), you're probably also going to be negative about Company B. That's not the kind of person we want to hire. There is absolutely no reason for you **not** to be upbeat about the military. Be positive.

Say, instead, "The military has helped me develop my leadership skills and my ability to organize, manage time effectively, take difficult objectives and accomplish them." This statement is a positive response about the military.

Then you could say, "I really feel that I can improve the quality of my life by moving into Corporate America. What we're really doing in the military every day is practicing — and hoping we never have to put into action what we're practicing. That is not a career objective that excites me."

I am not suggesting you use these words. I'm suggesting you follow this thought process. Throughout this book, I am not trying to put specific words in your mouth — I am trying to show you how to formulate your answers, how to formulate your **thought process.** We never want someone to take another's answer and use it literally.

**DON'T USE MY WORDS.
USE MY THOUGHTS.**

So, as you began to evaluate leaving the military, you considered your options. You might explain this by saying, "Corporate America became the absolute best option for me."

Tell us the reasons you want to come to Corporate America. What is it about Corporate America that excites you? Tell us you have abilities you're not practicing now in the military that will make an impact daily in a corporate environment.

Let us hear, for example, that you want to work for one of the best companies in the world — and that you're going to **improve** that company. Always "stretch the envelope" — taking an outstanding situation and improving it.

That's what we're looking for in a development candidate. We're not looking for people who fix things — who are problem-solvers in a negative environment. As a matter of fact, outstanding people are not interested in fixing. They don't want to take a system that had been excellent, then failed, and bring it back up — only to see it fail again. The outstanding person is someone who wants to "stretch the envelope." In other words, they want to take a situation and improve it beyond where it has ever been before. Most companies you will work for are companies that are very smooth running. They want people to help them grow and become even better.

Give this answer in two parts: first, your reasons for leaving the military, and then your reasons for coming to Corporate America. We want people who are motivated by **positive** change, not negative change. It is important that you give **specific** reasons for both of these questions.

Don't be naive. You won't love every job you'll have, but we expect you to work through jobs that aren't the greatest with a strong attitude and outstanding performance.

What Have You Gained From Your Time In The Military?
You're frequently going to be asked, "What have you gained from your time in the military?" It amazes me how applicants

brush off this question — one of the most loaded questions you're going to get. As I often tell applicants, "Let's take a look at this. Roger Cameron only recruits military officers, so we could draw the hypothesis that a company coming to Roger Cameron to hire knows they're going to hire a military officer." It must mean they're coming to me because they want a military officer. Therefore, it must mean they're wanting military officers because of what officers have gained from military experiences. That makes sense to me. Therefore, you must unload.

You can respond, "Where do I begin? I have developed the ability to prioritize, organize, effectively manage my time, accomplish difficult objectives, work with a variety of different people, and work in different atmospheric environments — the desert, the mountains, and the cold areas. I've learned how to perform tough objectives regardless of what the climatic conditions are. I've learned how to take difficult objectives and break them down into component parts and how to motivate subordinates to accomplish those objectives, getting tough jobs done with minimum assets of equipment and dollars." My point is — you have to unload. Recruiters have to feel you really have gained something from your time in the military. You may brush it off by saying, "Well, I've gained maturity," or "I've gained the ability to manage assets and people." That's not enough. Be careful how you answer this question.

Answering The "Why" Questions

"Why" is the most frequently asked question facing a military officer. I have to remind you that we're looking for development candidates. Development candidates are ultimately going to spend the bulk of their days making decisions. We ask the word "Why" to determine how you think and how you reason and to see your ability to come to a quality

conclusion. The recruiter will listen to how you thought through the steps along the way and how you came to a conclusion in your mind.

Remember that both you and the company want you to go as high as you can in management. Top managers are primarily paid for their ability to reach a quality conclusion. Allow us inside your mind — as you talk about how you came to a certain conclusion. We want a manager who does independent thinking — who makes decisions based on his/her own thinking rather than on a recommendation from someone else.

"Why" is a word attached to numerous key subjects. Why did you choose that college? Why that curriculum? Why the military? Why that branch of the military? Why do you want this position?

The best approach to any **"Why"** question is to think in terms of a **comparison.** Compare the positives and negatives of the choice you made with the positives and negatives of your other options — concisely, **without** rambling.

Tell us, for example, the options you had in financing college — borrowing money from family members or a bank, getting work, or winning a scholarship. You planned on ROTC being a big part of your college career. Let us know you analyzed all those factors before you came to a decision. I often ask military officers why they chose ROTC. The most frequent response I get is because they had no other way to earn their way through college. That is to suggest to the recruiter that if you can't get into ROTC, you can't graduate from college. Well, I just don't agree with that. There are other ways to finance your education.

I sometimes ask applicants whose major was history why they chose this field. A typical response is, "Well, I thought I wanted to go to law school." My reply is, "But, you're not a lawyer." The applicant says, "Well, ROTC came along and with that, I had an obligation to the military." I say, "Well, what happened to the objective of being a lawyer?" The reply is that the applicant changed his/her mind. Now, wait a minute. This applicant spent four years gearing up to be a lawyer, and walked away from the objective. No, I really don't think so. It's just that the applicant was unwilling to let me see how his/her mind functions. I don't have a choice but to walk away from that applicant. So, understand the critical nature of your ability to handle a **"Why"** question. Many recruiters will give you nothing but a **"Why"** interview. The key here is to let us know each step. And, in telling this to the recruiter, be succinct. Don't ramble.

An excellent exercise is to take all the major events in your life and write them down. Then, put the word **"Why"** in front of each. Talk out your answers, your analysis, on a tape recorder. Next, listen to yourself. Does what you say show strong reasoning? When it does, you're in good shape for interviewing.

Answering Education Questions
If you have a degree that is generally considered irrelevant to business, such as liberal arts, the question is not whether you should or should not have chosen it. The question is, how do you sell it to Corporate America? You and I both know that some of the top people in Corporate America have liberal arts degrees. But, I've never had a company ask me to find them an individual with a degree in liberal arts. It's perfectly all right that you have one. No one would suggest that you couldn't get value out of it. Yet, it's irrelevant to the functions in Corporate America. You'll have to handle it in an interview.

Don't get defensive about your liberal arts degree. We're not suggesting you wasted your time in college or that you're not going to get value from it. However, it seems I spend half my time consoling people who have this degree. I want to help you get over the fact that it is an irrelevant degree — it was not designed for Corporate America, for the world of profit. It isn't related to finance, data processing, engineering, business, accounting, etc. — those areas directly linked to Corporate America.

That doesn't mean it's bad. But, it does mean that you'll need months to find a company looking for a liberal arts degree as you go through *The Wall Street Journal*. You'll also have to handle it in an interview.

Here's a suggestion to explain it: "Relative to my decision today to come into Corporate America, my liberal arts degree was a mistake. I don't want to suggest that I didn't get things out of political science that will be of value to me because I thoroughly enjoyed it and feel I developed skills important in the business world, such as problem-solving and communication skills. However, had I known then what I know today, of my desire to have a career in the profit-oriented world, I would have earned a relevant degree."

Stress your determination to enter the business world. Frequently, in asking a person with an irrelevant degree why they want to go into business, we have to say, "You've never shown any indication of interest in business in the 25+ years of your life."

I draw the analogy that you have a neighbor who has been next door for 26 years. You've left the house every morning, returned every night — but never looked across the fence and said hello. Then, suddenly, one day, you lean across the fence and ask the neighbor to marry you. The neighbor answers, "For 26 years you've ignored me. Now you want to marry me. Why?" The neighbor has every reason to ask — and you need to explain. Give proof and evidence. You can't just say, "Sally no longer has an interest in me; therefore, I'm coming to you."

You're going to have to tell Corporate America how you decided you wanted a career in industry. Give proof and evidence of research you did, books you read, people you interviewed, choices you considered — **why** you've concluded you want to have a career in the business world.

I remember being in Fort Bragg, North Carolina, interviewing an officer with a government degree. I said, "Government degree. I just don't know what I can do." He said, "I'm coming to Corporate America whether through you or through someone else. I want to use your company because you have placed four of my friends." He then went on to give me very solid **proof and evidence** of his interest. "The reason I'm coming to Corporate America is I have talked with friends in major corporations and read several books (he stated title and author) about business which have encouraged me to make this choice. For the following reasons (he put his hands up in the air and ticked them off), I have decided to go into Corporate America." I listened to him. There was absolutely no question in my mind this young man had done his homework. He was committed and convincing. I brought him to the conference, and every company fought over him. He now has an outstanding job in industry, is performing at a remarkable level, and has remained a close friend and ally of mine.

Recruiters don't care whether you have an irrelevant degree. They **do** care whether you are coming to us for the right reasons. You're bringing us **proof and evidence** of those reasons, not simply rhetoric.

Accomplishments Deserve Full Answers

As I have previously stated in developing your resume, **no question will be more important than, "Tell me about a significant accomplishment."** After all, if you can't talk about past accomplishments, there is no reason to believe you can talk about future accomplishments. Normally, the way the question will be asked is this: "Tell me about a significant accomplishment and how you accomplished it." Be very careful to answer all three parts of this key question about an accomplishment.

Often, when I ask an applicant this question, I'll wait two or three minutes to find out what the accomplishment actually is! **Identify** the accomplishment in your **opening** statement. The example you give should be an accomplishment with an **impact** on your mission. Take the time to **develop the significance.** Tell how your accomplishment had a major effect on the overall status of the mission. I encourage you to use numbers (quarterly) to help show significance. "My command of 120 soldiers and 480 combat vehicles . . . ."

Don't tell the recruiter, "What I did was important." Don't use the word **significant.** **Show** that it was important and significant by your answer. Your answer should **demonstrate** the accomplishment.

I remember a trip I made to Germany to do some final interviewing. I had sent letters to approximately 30 applicants asking them to be prepared to tell me about a significant accomplishment, why it was significant, and how they accomplished it. No applicants work harder to prepare than applicants from Germany. They understand they do not have the luxury of putting in their resignations after they interview. They come to the United States extremely well-prepared. But, this was interesting: as hard as they worked, I did not have one applicant get this question right. Not one. Every one wanted to tell me what the accomplishment was and then tell me how they accomplished it. No one took the time to elaborate on the **significance** of the accomplishment itself.

One young man in field artillery said to me, "Roger, I was given the task of designing a new firing system for our field artillery unit." I said, "Insignificant issue." He said, "Roger, I've got to tell you something. If that's insignificant, I have never done anything significant." I said, "Why don't you let me try it?" I continued, "This event occurred while I was stationed in Germany (we consider that to be the most eastern defensive line of the United States). If we were going to run into a conflict at that time, it was probably going to come from across the Russian border. My job was to design a new firing system. In the event of a conflict, it is the field artillery's job to put steel on the target accurately before we get run over. If we don't put steel accurately on the target, that is exactly what will happen." You see, if he had established this, I could have seen the importance of what he was doing. But, he never even tried. He never took the effort to do so. You must take the responsibility to establish the significance of your accomplishments. After all, there are three parts of the question.

1) What is the accomplishment? Tell me immediately.
2) What is the significance of it?
3) Tell me how, in fact, you accomplished it.

As you explain how you accomplished a goal, you must give examples that illustrate your competencies as I have described in "Behavior And Basics" on page 185.

Once you see it, you realize that you can't simply **say** that it was important. We in Corporate America are not going to buy the rhetoric — we want to see the explanation of its importance, difficulty, or significance.

Your answer should show that you

- Were organized
- Knew priorities
- Found solutions to unexpected problems
- Worked well with peers, superiors, and subordinates
- Managed time effectively
- Were goal oriented
- Were able to break a goal down into parts, assigning those parts to subordinate managers, if necessary
- Brought the work to a conclusion. Be sure to mention if you brought the project in on budget and/or on time — and how that had an **impact on the mission.**

Don't be in a rush to answer this crucial question. It's one of the most important questions you'll be asked in an interview. And, you **will** be asked. You can be certain that you'll be asked for **numerous** examples.

Problem Solving
A similar question is, "Tell me about a significant **problem** you solved. Why was it significant, and how did you solve it?" Usually, this doesn't mean a people problem. It's a problem that had impact on the overall mission.

Reach back to pull out of your military career the most relevant problems and your most relevant accomplishments related to work performance.

Location Preference
What is your location preference? This question has probably caused more recruiters to get an instant bad attitude about an

applicant than any other. The most frequent answer is, "I'm open." But, "open" is **not** a definition of location. Recruiters don't believe it. **Don't use it.**

There are very few people in this world who are honestly open when it comes to a location preference. So, the first words from you in answering this key question must be a **regional** preference — the Northeast, the Midwest, the Southeast, etc. Don't give a city or a state; just specify a region. Give the broadest area possible — but one that honestly answers the question.

You may then want to follow the regional preference with a statement that you're open, saying, "I am not really looking for a location. I'm looking for a career. If everything is equal, then I would prefer the position to be in the Northeast. But, I have an enthusiastic attitude about going anywhere in the United States."

Be **smart**, as well as **honest**, in how you answer. If, for example, you're interviewing for a position in Cincinnati and your true preference is the Northeast, say your location preference would be east of the Mississippi River. That will include Cincinnati and the Northeast.

Never waste your time, or a company's time, by telling them something that is not true. If you're not willing to relocate, if you're not willing to be open, **then say so.** Analyze what you're willing to do. Be honest about it — with yourself and with interviewers. However, if you're wanting a career with a *FORTUNE 500* company, you must be willing to relocate. **Do not assume you can take the good and reject the bad.** When most companies are national/international and hiring an individual to become a top manager, it only makes sense that you be willing to relocate.

Applicants sometimes say they have a great attitude about going anywhere in the United States with the exception of California and New York. I say to them that those are the two highest gross national product areas in the country. It doesn't make sense that you, as a development candidate, can eliminate the locations that produce the greatest dollar volume for your company. This doesn't mean you're going to have to live there your entire career, or even move to those states. But, we can't assure you this won't happen. Applicants have also told me, "I want to live in the geographical area of my preference, and later I would be willing to move." "I have been on a remote assignment and haven't been near my parents for two or three years." "I want to go there to begin my career." We've heard those statements a million times. Once we have put you in that location, you don't have more reason to leave after two or three years; you have more reason to stay. Officers before you have made this a negative situation for most major corporations.

On the other hand, we have a great attitude about putting you where you want to be if we get a strong feeling that you are willing to go anyplace. You must be honest not only with yourself, but with Corporate America. You must analyze exactly what it is that will allow you to accomplish the objectives you want, and proceed to the type of company that allows you to accomplish those objectives.

Be sure you speak with everyone who will be a part of your career decision. After your recruiting firm and interviewing companies have spent time and money to assist in your transition or to hire you, it is very unprofessional to tell them your spouse, fiancé (fiancée), or parents do not want you to leave a certain geographical area. Be a responsible person and discuss relocation with those involved in the decision before, not after, you engage a recruiting firm or a company. To hope that everything will work out "perfectly" is immature and irresponsible decision making. Our firm and our company clients are hostile about this — and rightfully so. The time to think about this is before you interview, not afterwards.

Your Leadership/Management Style
Companies don't just come to the military officer for a college degree. They can get that from any campus. They come to you for what they **can't** find on just any campus — the combination of your degree and your **proven leadership ability.**

You will be asked in every interview, **"What is your leadership style?" You can either be prepared for it or you can be ruled out — your choice.** I can hear you now. "Oh, Roger, I'll have no problem when I get into the interview to explain what my leadership style is." Give it a try now — walk in the other room, grab a tape recorder, and instantly verbalize your leadership style. Easy? I rest my case. It makes no difference whether you stay in the military four years or 104 years. No one in the military will ever ask you what your leadership style is. They will simply observe it.

Realize that the question, "What is your leadership style?" can come in many forms. For example, "How do you motivate people to accomplish objectives?" "Why do your people want to work for you?" "How do you lead?"

Now, all of a sudden, you're coming to Corporate America. You answer nine out of 10 interview questions perfectly, but you can't answer the question which is **most** important for hiring a military officer: How do you motivate subordinates? Obviously, then, you're not going to be successful in getting through an interview. Under no circumstance can you give us book answers. You cannot tell us you lead by example, are a situational manager, or manage by objective. This simply is not adequate. We want to know **what you do** to motivate subordinates.

Describe your leadership/management style in your own words — and show how it's been effective for you. In listening to your answer about your leadership style, recruiters want to lean back in their chairs, close their eyes, and through your verbal picture of your leadership style, envision you going through your day motivating subordinates in their company. The key is to give details. For instance, start with the objective you are given. "When I'm given an objective, the first thing I do is take some quiet time to analyze the objective to determine what I'm being asked to do and to identify the time frame for accomplishing it. Then, I bring in my subordinate managers. We sit in front of my desk in a circle. I **explain** to them (notice I don't say I **tell** them) what the objective is and the time frame we have to get it done. Now, I ask them for their input (participative management) as to how they see us accomplishing these objectives. I do this primarily because they are frequently closer to the job than I am, and they usually have very definite ideas as to how to accomplish this objective in minimum time."

> ## DON'T USE MY WORDS.
> ## USE MY THOUGHTS.

In other words, what you are doing is **listening**. Often, as officers tell me their leadership style, here are the words I hear most frequently: "I **tell** my people what our objective is. I **tell** them the time frame. I **tell** them . . . ." Sometimes, I just want to say to them, "Don't you ever shut up and **listen?**" Participative management is making **everybody** feel they are part of the decision. I defy you to convince anyone that they are part of the decision when you are doing nothing but **telling**. We would like to think that you **do** listen to what subordinates have to say. **Be careful.** The administrative part of your answer should be seconds to a minute long. We are much more interested in your motivational ability, which should constitute 80% of your answer. We feel we could do the administration by memo, so keep it to a minimum.

As you motivate subordinates to accomplish these objectives, how do you do it? Are you a positive motivator? If you are, tell me succinctly how you positively motivate? I want to hear such things as, "Often, I call my first sergeant and express my thanks for putting in a 14-hour day, for getting the job done, and for bringing it in ahead of time. Sometimes, I'll pull a troop right out of the line in front of everybody else." You see, I can envision you doing that. But, you have to explain this to me. Too many military officers are totally lazy in giving detail. They do not want to explain **specifically** how they do it. There are many "leaders" in the military, but darn few **motivators**. We want motivators. You must be able to tell us if you do it and how you do it — specifically.

Think through all the situations when you've worked with a difficult individual. Such individuals have forced you to find creative ways to motivate them. Write out what the circumstances of these situations were, what was difficult, and what you did to change and motivate the subordinate. Put down at least five experiences. You'll start to see a pattern in these situations — why you've been successful as a leader. Get a good handle on this — as it points to your leadership style.

I want to alert you to an issue that has developed since the original publication of *PCS*. Most recruiters today are adamant about hiring individuals who have the ability to "change behavioral patterns" in subordinates. The specific issue is, do you have the ability to develop your subordinates to continue enhanced performance after you have left the scene? Too often, we suspect by your comments that as long as you're there to "motivate," your subordinates will produce. It is important for you to demonstrate that you enhance/change behavioral patterns to give permanent substantive improvement to your subordinates.

Too often, officers say they have a "flexible" style (which is a book answer). In other words, depending on the situation, they use different management styles. But, if you say this, you're actually admitting you are controlled **by** the situation. The style of leadership will not **basically** change, but how you **modify** this style to fit a situation may change.

For example, with hard-nosed, difficult individuals, you **may** be more aggressive or forceful to motivate them. With others, it is better to give more encouragement or support, working them through a problem. Your **style** of leadership won't change — only the way you approach individuals.

Remember a number of key factors. Real leaders must

- **Be motivators**

- **Be trustworthy**

- **Be strategic thinkers**

- **Provide vision**

- **Be approachable**

- **Take care of their subordinates**

- **Change behavior patterns**

In conclusion, you must show where your style has gone beyond the guidelines that the military has given you. We're looking for how you professionally go beyond the guidelines. A development candidate is someone who, as I have mentioned, wants to "stretch the envelope" to allow a company to produce beyond where it has produced before. If we can't see that you individualized your leadership style, we will probably believe you don't individualize anything else. Details are most important. Don't ramble. Be specific. Be concise and articulate.

Explaining The Handling Of Specific People Problems
You will be asked to give **numerous** examples of specific people problems you have solved as a leader in the military. It is critically important that you give us problems that are **performance** oriented. In other words, we would have **no** interest in alcohol, family, drugs, or financial issues. While I realize this wipes out about 70% of what you do in the military, those are problems that rarely happen in Corporate America. Consequently, they are not good examples to give to a recruiter. We want performance-oriented problems. You must use an example of someone you supervise directly, such as an NCO working for you who couldn't prioritize, organize, or problem solve. You worked with this individual who was a good worker and had a great attitude about coming to work, but just couldn't quite accomplish his/her objectives. Through your personal leadership and motivation, you turned this average performer into a better performer.

When I ask this question, frequently, applicants give me an example of a specific people problem they solved by terminating the persons. They either sent the individuals to another unit or forced them to leave the military. This suggests that their leadership style **failed**. Why would they give us an example of a problem they solved in which their leadership failed? This is beyond my comprehension. Had I asked them for an example of a people problem which they failed to resolve, then I would have expected them to give me this answer. We are looking for military officers who have the ability to take a people problem and resolve it in a **positive** fashion. As a result, we have a better performer due to behavioral enhancement.

Do You Micro-Manage?

Many people miss the rather subtle point made by this question. If you said "no" to this question, I would have to tell you that none of my companies would hire you. This statement bewilders many people. Let me explain. First of all, I didn't ask if you were a micro-manager. If I were to ask you that, I would hope you would say, "No." My definition of a participative manager is someone with a "steel rod backbone wrapped in a soft exterior." A recruiter can see the soft exterior, but has to ask questions to determine your backbone — questions such as, "Do you micro-manage?" Your response to this question would hopefully be similar to this: "Yes — on rare occasions," or "Yes, but very infrequently," or "Yes, one or two times in my career my commander has given me a 'hot potato' and a short response time. You bet I was looking over everyone's shoulder to ensure mission success." You are in Corporate America. We do not have a perfect world. There will be times your company will need you to handle crisis situations. They will want to know you have handled them in the military. I remember an incident at one of our conferences when a recruiter was discussing one of my applicants who he had interviewed that morning. He said, "I sure like him. He is bright, intelligent, poised — an excellent communicator. As a matter of fact, if I had a daughter, I would hope she would marry someone just like him." I was feeling very proud until he said, "However, Roger, I'm not going to be able to recommend our company hire him because he has never had his back against the wall — he has never had to manage a crisis situation. And, you know our company has its fair share of problems on occasion." No matter how hard I tried to persuade him to reconsider, it was too late. The applicant failed to recognize (or didn't actually listen to) the intent of the question. He heard the word "micromanage" and immediately tried to distance himself from it.

To Be A Fair Manager, Must You Use Negative Motivation?
Your immediate response is probably **"no."** If I ask if the military mandates by written policy that you use negative motivation, you again would probably respond with a resounding "no." However, I'll prove to you that both answers should be "yes." Let's say you work for me. One morning you come to work, and I tell you to clean out your desk and leave. You say, "I beg your pardon." I reply, "I said you are finished; you are fired; you no longer work here. Clean out your desk and go home." Your response is, "Why?" And, I answer, "Well, there are two things you are not doing to the standard I expect." Your reply is, "Well, Roger, why didn't you tell me?" The response is exactly on target. If I had been a fair manager, I would have called you into my office and explained that while you were doing many things right, there were two areas in which your skills were below acceptable standards. I might suggest that I would give you 30 days to bring the first area up to standard and 60 days to bring the second to standard. Also, I would offer to help you in any way I could. In essence, I have **counseled** you — which is what a fair manager would do. It is also what the military mandates in counseling. Counseling **is** negative motivation. While it is delivered in a positive manner, let me assure you people do not come to counseling sessions feeling it is for positive motivation. Unfortunately, when I mention negative motivation, officers too often think of actions that involve shouting and commanding. I do not feel this is any form of motivation. Instead, it is a **fear** driven management style. That's okay when you have Fort Leavenworth to back you up. Using "fear tactics" in Corporate America will

cause you to have a short career. Be sure you reflect before instantly heading off in the wrong direction.

What Are Your Long- And Short-Term Career Goals?

This question is frequently asked. While your answer is important, the delivery is equally important. The question is really a communication question. In front of audiences, I have asked this question. I have yet to have anybody answer it properly. Purposely, the recruiter gives you a question with vagueness in it. Did you notice there is no definition for long or short? Unless you describe what these two words mean to you, how can we evaluate your answer?

You might tell me that your short-term goal is to become familiar with your position, to get your feet on the ground, or to feel comfortable with what you're doing. If my definition of short-term is two years, I will think you are pretty slow. You may have it in your mind that short is two months, so do not answer the question until you give the recruiter your definition of long or short. Do **not** ask recruiters for their definition. Provide your own.

Before you interview, think about your short-term goals. Write down at least five things you want to accomplish (both in your personal life and professional life) within the next year.

Think about your long-term goals. Write down five things you want to accomplish within the next five, ten, fifteen, or twenty years.

Now, beginning with your short-term goals, outline the goals and how you plan to reach those goals. Break down each goal into reachable increments. What are the intermediate steps you need to accomplish along the way? Establish a time frame for the realistic accomplishment of each goal and use a calendar to remind yourself of each step to be taken. Do a similar, but broader, outline for your long-term goals. What short-term goals can you use to reach each long-term goal? Some goals may span 12 months, others several years. Think about how each goal fits into and affects the big picture of your life.

By completing this exercise, **you will discover how attainable your goals really are, and you will have a clear picture of your own achievements.** Whether in the military or in business, you will find this to be rewarding and excellent preparation for attacking all projects and challenges.

This exercise will assist you in identifying and expressing the process you use to establish and attain goals and objectives. It will also provide you with examples of goals you have set and how you accomplished them.

It is important that you be aware of how industry will analyze and judge your goals and accomplishments. Your goals and objectives should stretch you and "make you perspire" while reaching them. Industry feels the more **difficult** the objective, the more **significant** the achievement. You will need to prove to companies you have the ability to meet their expectations by giving them examples of goals and objectives you have set and met, and yet did so by overcoming difficult obstacles.

Why Should I Hire You?
Let's say a company has a single opening and has interviewed three or four candidates. They all look good. Then comes the question — why should they hire you?

If you could get inside a recruiter's mind, he or she is really asking, "Why should I hire you **versus** the other candidates

I'm considering?" The answer I get from applicants is always the same: "I'm the person who can get the job done. I have the credentials to do the job." That's what **everyone** says — and it really doesn't **impact** or make an impression.

I am impressed with an applicant who says, "Roger, I'm sure the kind of people you're interviewing all have good abilities. All of us are confident we can do the job. But, let me tell you something I have that I feel is an integral part of me. You won't find anyone with a better **attitude.**"

This applicant further explains, "If I need to be here at 6:00 A.M. to get the job done, I'll be here. If I need to work through my lunch hour, I'll be here. If I need to work late, I'll be here. You don't have to worry whether or not I'm going to be here — I **will be.**" And, "I'll be here with a positive attitude," this candidate continues. "Anytime you need anything done, give it to **me.** I'll get it done for you. That's what **separates me** from the other applicants." I honestly believe the **desire to apply one's ability** and a positive attitude about doing it is more important than just **having** the ability.

You must answer the question, "Why should I hire you?" with words that have **unique** impact. I've heard it again and again over the years: "I can get the job done. I have the credentials." But, I've rarely heard anyone make an impression by telling me what makes them special and unique.

And, don't go on and on. You'll become boring and lose the recruiter. I remember interviewing an applicant at Fort Sill, Oklahoma. He'd been asked six times why he wanted sales — and six times he tried to explain. He could have made real impact by using fewer words, such as, "I am **going** to have a career in sales. While I'd like to have the opportunity to have the sales position with your company, I want to assure you, I

will have it with some high-quality company." Of course, it is important that you say this in a positive manner and not in an antagonistic one.

This situation is similar to an officer listening to an NCO try to explain why a job wasn't done right. The more the NCO talked, the more he knew how guilty he was, and so did his superior. He could have said simply, "I didn't accomplish the objective. I understand what I did wrong. It won't happen again."

Don't explain and continue to explain. It's so much easier to punch with a **few** words versus **many**. And, remember: When you're asked why you want a career in Corporate America, be emphatic. Give proof and evidence. Put credibility in your answer.

I like to hear an applicant say, "Roger, I **am** going to have a career in Corporate America." I rarely hear words like these. Your answer will have impact based on the solid research and clear thinking you've done. You've reached a conclusion and can verbalize it. Remember — you must back up your statements with **proof and evidence**.

The Negative Interview
The negative interview is designed to test your conviction about career objectives. Companies feel that if they can talk you out of what you want to do, they have proven you have less conviction. Particularly in the area of manufacturing, we might see the question, "What is your opinion of shift work?" In other words, we have had people leave manufacturing in Corporate America because they didn't like shift work. It's pretty hard to go into an interview and say, "I'm really excited about shift work." But, one of your early promotion levels in manufacturing may be to manage a 24-hour operation. Different shift times create unique problems. They have their own

idiosyncrasies in motivating subordinates to perform. If you know one of your early lines of promotion is to manage a 24-hour operation, then, obviously, it would be better to have experienced those different shifts yourself. We also know many of you coming out of the military have not been able to get your masters degree because of the amount of time TDY, down range work in the field, deployment, etc. Many times, you can get a better quality MBA during daytime hours than in the evening. Sometimes, going on shifts early in your career is an ideal way for you to work toward your masters degree.

When recruiters attempt to talk you out of a job, they may use different tactics, such as, "Well, you're an outstanding candidate, and I really feel our company should hire you. However, I feel you would be better suited for position A than the position for which you are interviewing." You've got to fight them. Many times, they're simply testing your ability to be committed to and convinced about the position for which you are interviewing. This is what we call the negative interview. For instance, if you are applying for a sales position, they might say, "Sales — I think you have strong poise and self-confidence, but you have to understand, with sales you're going to get a lot of negative aspects within a day. Someone may be slamming the door on you or canceling an appointment at the last minute when you're already in your car driving there. You're going to end up wasting some time in a day. It's very difficult for you to get organized and to effectively manage your time. However, I believe you have the ability in our company to handle different positions which are equally outstanding. I would like to refer your resume to other departments. Would you like me to do that?" Again, they may simply be attempting to determine your conviction. Be careful!

A couple of companies, in the follow-up interviewing process, have a designated negative interviewer whose sole purpose is to try to talk you out of the job you're seeking. Unfortunately, not all applicants have listened to me, and they have allowed a company to talk them out of the job. I've actually had applicants come back to me and say, "Roger, I remember what you said, but I'm confident that's not what the company was doing. They actually thought I was better for something else." I moaned! Then, true enough (as I get feedback), they were ruled out for lack of conviction. As a military officer, you're coming out three to eight years behind your age group. If you're going to enter the race at that point, you must be committed. You **must** have conviction. You **must** know what you want. You **must** be able to focus and concentrate on that objective. Don't let somebody sway you within 30 seconds of an interview.

Occasionally, the negative interview is used to determine poise and self-confidence. Sometimes, recruiters use it "to push on the end of your nose" to see what reaction they'd get. While this is rarely used in interviewing today, I want to at least make you aware of it. Normally, the type of negative questions you will hear will be, " A 3.5 grade point average — why wasn't it better?" First of all, you will usually find the recruiter asking a negative question on a **positive** point. In other words, it isn't for the purpose of embarrassing you. It is for the purpose of determining how you handle a negative situation. In Corporate America, just like in the military, you will not always be in a positive situation. There will be times you'll be in combative meetings. You will have to defend your viewpoint. We want to see if you have gained the maturity in the military to be able to do so. Do your neck and ears turn red? Do you put on the boxing gloves? Or, do you simply square the shoulders, look the recruiter in the eye, and handle it positively? It will potentially come up in interviews. Always remember, the objective is not to embarrass, but to determine poise and self-confidence. Be determined.

Behavior And Basics

The behavioral interview is being used more and more and is an effective tool for evaluation. The goal of the interview is to uncover the applicant's behavioral traits, those skills or characteristics that the applicant applies consciously or unconsciously to accomplish objectives. **(Do not attempt to go through this exercise until you have completed your work in Chapter 3 in "Objective/Subjective Assets.")** Some companies refer to this interview as the "basic characteristics interview"; others call it the "competency-based" interview. In this interview, the recruiter listens to your illustrations of previous experiences to identify characteristics integral to a successful development candidate.

Most companies have determined the behavioral traits that they consider a successful employee must possess. Not surprisingly, companies' lists are very similar.

Today, it's taboo for you to actually state the trait. You can't say, for example, that you're "intelligent and competitive." As I have previously stated, you must illustrate these characteristics verbally by discussing your past accomplishments.

How will you know in an interview when a recruiter is looking for **your** behavioral traits? The recruiter will ask you **how** you did something. Anytime you hear a recruiter ask, **"How?"** let it be a signal to you that you need to give examples of your competencies used in accomplishing goals or the problem resolution. The recruiter might say, "Tell me about an accomplishment and **how** you achieved it," or "Tell me about a problem you encountered and **how** you solved it."

To prepare for the behavioral interview, start by finding a quiet spot and analyzing exactly **how you** accomplish difficult objectives. This isn't a five-minute job. I envision it taking you a full day — or even more. As you examine your past accomplishments, make a list of those **common** behavioral traits (competencies, characteristics) that appear in situation after situation. Note how some traits are automatic, or subconscious, and how others require a conscious effort on your part. List the traits that appear frequently and cause outstanding performance. This is a key point. The trait should be developed to a level that results in exceptional achievement; otherwise, the list is meaningless to you. We all organize, manage our time, and interact with others, but do we do it to the degree that we would be considered outstanding in each trait?

Next, I would suggest you prioritize your list of traits and keep them firmly in mind with examples of accomplishments. As a result, in an interview, you'll be armed with the information about your most outstanding traits in order to give the recruiter a concise, articulate description.

Try this exercise to help you identify the traits you possess that you feel are most noteworthy. Lean back in your chair, close your eyes, and visualize an individual who has worked with you or for you and whose performance was outstanding. Think about what you most admired about that individual's performance. I have asked applicants to do this in interviews, and they have consistently mentioned the same characteristics. The individual they describe is always a hard worker, has a positive attitude, is goal-oriented, and is a team player. Now, think about the traits you have identified and which of those you think would describe you as well. Think about situations that have occurred in which you have used these outstanding traits and accomplished your goals to an exceptional degree. Use the tape recorder to record your answer.

Another exercise that may help you determine your personal traits is to pick up the phone and assume the role of a corporate recruiter calling Roger Cameron at Cameron-Brooks, Inc., Professional Recruiting Firm, asking me to recruit development candidates for you. Describe the behavioral traits you expect these individuals to possess. Again, you will see recruiter after recruiter asking for similar competencies.

Additionally, Appendix C contains a list of behavioral traits. Use this list to help you identify those characteristics you think best describe your strengths.

The following are types of characteristics recruiters want to see in a behavioral answer:
- Success-driven, goal-orientated, make-it-happen attitude
- Effective use of time
- Successful interaction with peers, superiors, and subordinates
- Organizational ability
- Prioritization
- Pre-problem solution ability
- Creativeness
- Innovativeness
- Competitiveness
- Sense of urgency
- Effective, persuasive communication
- Team player mentality
- Technical competency
- Strong work ethic

Record your significant accomplishments or problems solved on tape, and then listen to your answers. Remember, we're **not** looking for you to say, "I was goal-oriented. I effectively used my time." We need to hear a description of the action you took to see how you resolve a problem and accomplish an objective.

The behavioral traits interview is being used more and more and is considered one of the finest interviews given. A recruiter knows the specific traits the company wants. Be certain to prepare well for the interview. You can't count on the answers coming naturally. If they don't come out of your mouth on your tape recorder, they're not going to come out of your mouth in an interview.

STOP!

DON'T READ FURTHER UNTIL YOU HAVE RECORDED SIGNIFICANT ACCOMPLISHMENTS AND ANALYZED YOUR ANSWERS.

See Appendix D for an Interview Self-Evaluation Sheet you can use to evaluate your performance after each interview.

CHAPTER 7

Considering The Reasons For Rejection

"Roger Cameron is the MASTER of professional recruiting. He is direct and demanding! His methods produce unequaled success for every candidate willing to apply his techniques for corporate interviewing. This book is for all officers committed to making the transition to Corporate America. If you think you can obtain a promising new career without reading this book, you are obviously not committed. The person conducting your interview has studied it with great care."

— Warren Hubler
Safety Manager
Helmerich & Payne
International Drilling Co.

Considering The Reasons For Rejection

The following are actual comments from interviewers describing applicants who were declined. You will notice that some of the points are similar, but these similarities only emphasize their importance. The comments are grouped under four categories: preparation, communication, energy level, and leadership qualities.

Preparation

- **Lacked conviction; was difficult to hear.** So often, recruiters say, "Roger, I like everything the applicant said, but I'm not convinced that she meant what she said." Sometimes, we have applicants tell us they have consistently been soft-spoken. Their parents and teachers have often asked them to speak up, but they feel that it is natural for them to speak softly and that there is nothing they can do about it. I have found it helpful for applicants to use a tape recorder to correct this problem. Place the recorder across the room from you, and then project your voice into it without yelling. Do this for an hour every day. You may read from a book or pick a subject and spontaneously give a speech on it. The point is to project your voice. Don't cheat. Don't place the microphone so it is easier for the recorder to pick up the sound. Buy an inexpensive tape recorder rather than the best machine. The key is not to get a recorder that will pick up a weak voice. The test is to project your voice so that soon it will become natural for you to speak in a forceful, convincing manner.

You do not have to be soft-spoken for the rest of your life. I am not suggesting that you transform from someone who is mild-mannered and soft-spoken into someone who is loud and obnoxious. I am talking about presenting yourself in a professional and convincing manner. Watch people you know — for example, some of your superiors and other officers who have voices to which you respond positively — and watch how they project. Listen to the tone and volume of their voices. If you determine after working on this independently for several weeks or months that this isn't doing the job, then don't be afraid to go for outside help. Go to a diction instructor — someone who can help you use your voice in a better manner — or take a speech course. Do not accept failure in increasing the power and the impact of your voice.

- **Well rehearsed, but not specific when probed**. The applicant talked in generalizations. For example, to the question, "How did you build teamwork?" he answered, "I build teamwork with my subordinates." This generalization is not acceptable to recruiters. The applicant should have given specific examples of how he built teamwork. Be sure to do your homework so that you can give specifics and evidence in answer to questions.

- **Too rehearsed — said what the recruiter wanted to hear**. The applicant showed by his answers that he was not a confident person. Recruiters are sharp. They will see right through a facade. Prepare. Don't give someone else's answers or deliver by rote. It will not work. You must prepare in advance to be yourself and to convince the recruiter that you are the right person for the job.

- **Couldn't articulate and give specific examples of accomplishments**. Had the applicant used her tape recorder before the interview and listened to herself, this probably would not have happened. You cannot be successful as a development candidate without quality preparation. No one can speak in a concise, articulate manner without hard work and preparation.

- **Textbook answers**. The applicant might have felt that by giving perfect answers, the recruiter would think he was perfect. If you're not comfortable enough or not prepared enough to be relaxed and be your smart self, the recruiter will see right through you. Would you bring someone into your company who you felt lacked confidence or, in fact, was a fake?

- **Bad questions**. This applicant showed lack of understanding of the position and career. If you've spent the necessary time to get information about the job and company, you'll be able to do some pre-work. Write out your questions before you interview and practice verbalizing them. During your interview, listen carefully to the recruiters so you will be able to formulate appropriate questions and respond intelligently to **their** answers to your questions.

- **Programmed answers**. Some applicants give answers that appear canned, even shallow. They need to recognize the importance of sincerity in their delivery. Do your homework in order to digest the information and deliver it in your own personal style.

- **Superficial answers**. The applicant gave answers indicating lack of depth, quality, self-insight, and comprehension. Be aware that recruiters are looking for these characteristics. They are the foundation of a development candidate.

- **Same questions as everyone else.** The applicant did not listen carefully and did not gather sufficient information to ask specific, relevant questions. You cannot ask generic questions. Your questions must be relevant to that company and that position. They must have a purpose.

- **No competencies.** The applicant didn't listen, understand, or comprehend the competency-based interview. You must verbally illustrate your key characteristics without naming them. This is not easy, but you must find the time to prepare for this type of frequent interview.

- **Could not relate background.** The applicant couldn't draw parallels from past performance. Be sure to study the position for which you are applying before you interview so that you are prepared to relate how your experience and skills can be applied to the job.

- **Was not flexible about location.** The applicant took one second to say he was open, but then spent five minutes talking about a preference. This contradiction made the recruiter question the applicant's believability. While being flexible about location may be difficult for you, it is important for you to be certain about your willingness to relocate. Be sure you have a positive, concise way to describe your position and stick to it. You appear to be indecisive otherwise.

- **Didn't know what she wanted to do.** The applicant didn't prepare for the interview by analyzing her knowledge, skills, achievements, and objective/subjective assets. She lacked quality self-insight. She may have thought she could wing it and talk off the top of her head. Be sure you do whatever it takes before the interview to know specifically how your achievements and skills relate to the career you are seeking. Employers want to know how you can contribute to their success. Be ready to tell them.

Communication

- **Rambled. Poor communicator.** The applicant tried to tell the recruiter too much. He ran out of time and appeared unfocused. You can decrease the chance that you will ramble when answering questions by spending quality time before the interview thinking about some typical questions that may be asked and how you can answer concisely. When you are asked a question during the interview, take a few seconds to organize your thoughts. Answer succinctly, but be careful not to give answers that are so abbreviated they have no substance.

- **Talked nonstop. Didn't listen and didn't relate the background.** The applicant didn't look for cues from the recruiter about how the delivery of his answers was being accepted. Be sensitive to the recruiter and listen to what he or she says in order to relate your background to the job and company requirements. To be a development candidate, you must actively reflect, organize, deliver, and then be quiet. Remember, 73% of an executive's time is spent listening. You want to be sure you exhibit this characteristic in the interview.

- **Too much slang.** The applicant didn't realize that using informal language is not acceptable in a job interview. Recruiters are turned off by slang or repeated words, such as "O.K.," "roger," "do you know what I mean," or "you know." Omit slang or repetitious words from your conversation.

- **Couldn't get anything out of her.** This applicant had difficulty discussing her background and qualifications in a pleasant, conversational style. You must relax in an interview and help the recruiter know the real you. To prepare for a discussion of your qualifications, write down what you feel are significant achievements you have made that point to relevant skills the position would require, and then practice verbalizing them. Next, practice "interviewing" with good friends and tell them that you want the "interview" to be relaxed, so they can help you achieve this goal by giving you suggestions. The point is not to memorize a canned speech, but to be familiar with major points you will want to make in the interview so you are not caught off guard with nothing to say. A recruiter will not pull information from you.

- **Not an open communicator.** The applicant was guarded in his manner and had trouble revealing his true self. If you have prepared adequately for your interview and have practiced with another person, you will have taken a big step in being able to talk openly with the interviewer.

- **Lectured.** The applicant didn't display a natural, easy-going communication style. You must speak with, not to, the interviewer. Strive to listen to the interviewer and to answer questions as succinctly as possible so you don't appear to be lecturing.

- **Didn't answer precise questions.** The applicant's rambling answer indicated she may not have listened to everything the recruiter stated in his question. You must actively listen to every word before answering a question and take the time to formulate a direct answer.

- **Overused first names.** The applicant called the interviewer by name too many times during the interview in an effort to establish a comfortable rapport. Names must be used in moderation. Calling someone by name three or four times during a forty-five minute interview is appropriate. It is also important to deliver the interviewer's name in a sincere and natural way.

- **Poor eye contact.** By not maintaining eye contact with the interviewer, the applicant gave the impression of low self-esteem and a lack of self-confidence. Be sure to do what it takes to establish and maintain eye contact with other individuals before you interview.

Energy Level
- **Didn't show interest.** The applicant had poor posture and slumped in the chair. She showed very little enthusiasm, both in her voice quality and the statements she made. Recruiters are looking for candidates who exhibit energy and enthusiasm for the job. Be prepared to convince them you are just such a person.

- **Not natural; too stiff.** The applicant was unable to relax and be natural. You should be able to carry on a two-way conversation in an easy, natural, and enthusiastic manner.

- **Obnoxious.** The applicant was overly aggressive. While it is important to be enthusiastic, it is also necessary to observe how the recruiter is reacting to your delivery. Be sensitive to any "tell-tale" signs of adverse reaction and adjust. Practice with others before you interview and get feedback about your style.

- **Reserved; low energy level.** This applicant may not have known the importance of selling himself. He needed to show his ability to handle many tasks which can only be done with lots of energy. To make a recruiter believe you can handle a job, you must be excited about the opportunity.

You must show enthusiasm and a high energy level. It makes no difference whether you are applying for a position in engineering, production planning, or finance. You are first and foremost a development candidate. You must project an image similar to that of the top 10% of all managers. As a leader, your attitude is contagious. Would you allow your team to be slow? Unenthusiastic? Bored? Not sharp? You must show your enthusiasm and prove you can go the extra mile.

- **Too intense.** The applicant was too uptight. He was not relaxed. Companies want professional, poised people. Whether you are in a sales or leadership role, people will respond better if you are relaxed. You must always be comfortable with a pleasant, professional sense of humor.

Leadership Qualities

- **Not a team player.** The applicant impressed the recruiter as being too authoritative. Companies demand a leader who can be a team captain rather than a dominating coach. Recruiters are looking for candidates who will be able to motivate workers by getting their trust versus being their boss. When you practice for the interview, write down examples of how you have been a team player in any of your school or work experiences. Refer to how you delegated authority and encouraged participation and why others responded to your style. Then, practice presenting these experiences out loud.

- **Good supervision, but limited success.** This applicant had leadership responsibility, but could not articulate how he had positively carried out his responsibilities and impacted on his team. Be prepared in the interview to discuss how your actions as a leader caused positive change and motivated your team to significant accomplishments.

- **No initiative. Simply a caretaker.** In a fast-paced environment of highly skilled workers, you must creatively solve problems on your own initiative. This individual seemed content with the status quo. It is easier to go through life as a follower. This is not what we're looking for in a development candidate. You must have the initiative to enhance performance without prompting from your superiors.

- **Unrealistic regarding promotion.** The applicant stated a requirement for promotion within the first six months. Nothing will scare away companies faster than for you to make unreasonable demands. It is important to be ambitious, but realistic. You must temper your expectations. There are many factors that must be considered for promotion. You will not be promoted overnight. Be realistic in self-evaluation and promotion opportunity relative to your abilities. Unrealistic expectations usually mean a person expects too much too soon. It is a hard long road to the top. To reach the top, the road must be filled with significant contribution.

I have given you the most prevalent reasons recruiters have ruled out particular applicants over the years. As you look at these reasons, note that you have total control over the majority of them. In most all cases, effective preparation would be very beneficial. It's a matter of speaking up with enthusiasm, listening actively, addressing the questions directly, giving substance to your answers, having accurate self-insight, and being concise in what you have to say. I would encourage you to study this section very carefully before going into any interview in order to remind yourself of these factors just prior to the interview itself.

Moving Toward The Job Offer

*"Roger Cameron is military officer recruiting. Now, his proven principles for success in the marketplace are finally down on paper. Intense and professional, Roger's training is designed for the serious officer. Read it; learn it; practice it — then choose the career **you want** after the military."*

> — Charles Collins
> Assistant Brand Manager
> Procter & Gamble

CHAPTER 8

Moving Toward The Job Offer

Dollars And Sense

When you're talking with a company and they ask what money you expect, don't tell them that you're open. You know you're not open. Every time an applicant says that to me, I say, "Fine, we'll pay you $20,000." All of a sudden, they're backpedaling, "Well, that's not reasonable." I reply, "It isn't reasonable that you tell me you're open."

I have yet to find an applicant who is honestly open on the subject of money. "What dollars are you expecting?" a recruiter will ask. I think the answer that turns off the interviewer the most is for you to give a figure and say you should be paid that because that's what you're making in the military. We **don't** base our compensation in Corporate America on what you're earning in the service.

So, how can we handle this question of money? Generally speaking, you're probably going to take a $1,000 to $2,000 pay cut, although not in every case. I've brought many officers into Corporate America who gained an increase.

It's interesting that one time I had an applicant explain to a recruiter that the reason he wanted X number of dollars was because that's what the military paid him. The recruiter said, "I'll tell you what I'll do. What you're asking is $2,000 higher than what we want to pay. However, I'll increase my offer by $2,000 so that you're getting paid the same amount—providing I can continue to pay you, over your career with us, what the military would pay you!" The applicant, of course, quickly backed out of that situation.

You can't have it both ways. You're going to have to transition from the military's compensation program to the compensation program of Corporate America. Let the recruiter know you understand that. It's okay to want a certain figure, to want to avoid going backwards in pay. But remember, our attitude in business is, "You're welcome to stay in the military — no need to come to industry."

"Money is important to me," you can say. "I want to get what I'm worth, but it's only one of many factors. I'm not going to take a job based solely on money. I'm going to take a job based on the quality of the company, the quality of the career path, the operating philosophy of the company, the location, benefits, travel, etc."

Then, I recommend giving a salary range of no more than $2,000 to $3,000 (between suggested salaries). Recruiters are not going to accept $30,000 to $40,000 or $40,000 to $50,000. When you went into the military, you were paid the same whether you graduated from a leading college with a top engineering degree and a high GPA or graduated from a much lesser school with an irrelevant degree and a poor GPA. You must realize that when you leave the military and come to Corporate America, we're going to take you back to the way it was when you graduated from college.

We're going to pay you based on credentials. Thus, you can't use what the military is paying you as a basis for entering business.

Your choice is simple.

1) You can stay in the military taking what the services pay, or

2) You can come to Corporate America where you are paid and promoted according to performance.

In the hiring process, you're going to be paid on the basis of credentials and your ability to persuasively communicate them. Research the marketplace. Determine what your value is to Corporate America. Set a fair market value — one appropriate for you and for Corporate America.

Transitional Concerns

We are often asked about career "security" in Corporate America. This is a fair question relative to the perception of security in the military. As more than one officer has stated, "I know I will get a pay check every month if I stay in the military."

To begin with, during the years I have recruited military officers, only one has been laid off for economic reasons and that one was rehired by the same company within a couple of weeks. You are being hired as a **development candidate.** The military, regardless of world conditions, continues to produce ROTC and academy graduates. The same is true in industry — if we cease to develop leaders, somewhere in the future, we will have a leadership void. No quality company would voluntarily get themselves into that situation.

You should also realize the tremendous expense of hiring a development candidate. Anytime a company incurs an "expense," it is never taken lightly. It is now estimated that a hiring mistake will cost more than $35,000 in the first six months! This cost is what causes a company to take an officer through such a rigorous series of interviews. In many companies, one "no" by **any** interviewer in their company will eliminate that individual from further consideration. As one *FORTUNE 100* company stated, "We don't hire two to see if one can make it. We hire **one** and put every resource we have into making sure the candidate succeeds."

While the above facts are a close guarantee of "security," we must point out that not unlike the military, Corporate America is also competitive. It is essential that you start your new career eager to succeed, to accomplish difficult objectives, and to work hard and smart. In my lifetime, I have yet to see someone successful in the military who couldn't become successful in Corporate America. The tools of success are the same regardless of the profession.

Another area of concern is the physical transition itself. Many times, officers have unnecessary anxieties about this. You are going to find that your company will virtually walk you through each step. Normal procedures include flying both the new employee and spouse on a house or apartment hunting trip very soon after the hire. While all companies are different, generally speaking, you will also be given guidance on realtors, financial institutions, and neighborhoods. And, of course, all normal expenses will be paid. **Always** remember, each company has its own policies, and before you create an expenditure, you should determine if it is reimbursable. Also, your company normally covers all expenses that the military doesn't cover in the moving of your furniture and car mileage. Our applicants have been extremely pleased with their companies' relocation benefits. Corporations know that relocations can cause frustration and unwanted anxieties, and they work hard to eliminate as many as possible.

It is always our desire to help you get answers to specific questions. We encourage you to talk with other officers who have already transitioned. Many times, it is comforting to speak with someone who has actually been "in your shoes."

Pay Raises
There are three ways you can get increased compensation in Corporate America.

- **Annual pay raise:** This raise is just what it says. It is granted annually. There is no specific formula as to how much you can expect in a year (even though some companies have a general formula measured on performance). In all cases, you'll be evaluated on both objective and subjective performance factors.

- **Promotional pay raise:** With a grade level or position level promotion, you will receive a pay raise.

- **Merit pay raise:** Merit pay raise is given for performance above the expected norms. This raise is obtainable; however, it is not easy to receive in a world of high-achievers.

In your first year in Corporate America, it would be unlikely for you to receive more than an annual increase. In your second year, it would not be unusual for you to receive one or more of the three increases in compensation. Again, remember that you will be paid and promoted according to your performance.

Being a typical American, you'll never ever get paid what you feel you're worth. I know individuals in industry who are being paid $300,000 a year, and they still feel they're being underpaid. That doesn't mean they don't wear a smile every day. It's just what human nature is all about. There is never an ideal world. You don't see outstanding performers at Mobil, IBM, Procter & Gamble, and DuPont attempting to get into the military. Corporate America takes very good care of its people. You earn it first, then it's given to you. You won't get it before you go out and earn it.

$3,000 Is A Crucial Figure

When a company does a follow-up interview with an applicant, that company will spend $3,000, on a national average, for a follow-up interview. That will be necessary to cover airline tickets, rental cars, taxis, hotels, and food. Beyond that is the major expenditure of management's time to interview.

By making yourself conscious of this $3,000, you can help a recruiter spend it. Recruiters, not unlike applicants, are selfish. Their primary concern, and rightly so, is their own career — not yours. Many times, recruiters are young people, willing to sit through numerous interviews. While they do, they're very aware that every time they say "yes" to a follow-up interview, they have, in fact, signed a company check for $3,000.

They're aware they can't sign too many of these checks and then have upper management decline applicants they've sent before their record starts to reflect on their credibility. Too many applicants forget this — or are simply unaware of it. You must help the recruiter feel good about spending $3,000 for the follow-up. You can do that by giving the best possible interview.

If I could get you to write anything on the back of your hand as you go to interviews, it would be this: $3,000. There is probably no factor that should motivate you more to be competitive during the interview than remembering that figure. I suggest you write it on the top of every page of your notes. Think it over. Put yourself in the recruiter's position. If **you** had $3,000 in your wallet, would you spend that money pursuing the individual you're interviewing?

Many companies, on this dollar amount alone, will eliminate an applicant. Today, more companies are sending two or more recruiters to interview at our conferences. They feel it is less expensive to get a second, and even a third, opinion at the conference. Then, when they fly out an applicant for follow-up interviews, they are more assured the other managers will agree with their opinions. It's a better decision and less costly to get multiple judgments at the conference **before** flying that applicant in for a follow-up interview. Also, it assures a higher rate of offer to follow-up ratio.

We're finding companies are increasingly aware of recruiting costs. **So, remember that $3,000 the next time you step in front of a recruiter**.

Don't Overspend
Be alert. Know what amounts you're billing to the company paying for your interview expenses. If you go to the hotel bar and order six drinks, you're showing poor judgment. My own judgment, as a company, would be to withhold any job offer.

Think, think, think. Don't be like the young man who traveled to Chicago to interview, then found he didn't have the $30 cash to pay taxi fare from the airport to the client's office. All he had was credit cards. So, he ordered a limousine for $120. You may say, "That was good judgment. He got himself to the company's office." But, let me assure you it was **poor** judgement to have the vice president of personnel see him pull up in a limousine, billed to the expense account. This applicant did **not** get an offer. The poor judgment started when the applicant didn't take a sufficient amount of cash with him for incidental costs. It is logical that you will have to take taxis.

Today, to travel on follow-up interviews with less than $100 in your pocket would be poor judgment.

A company is always measuring your judgment. From the time you leave your door, you're spending the company's money. You're going to be examined every step of the way. That applies to everything — flights, taxis, hotels, and dinners with company recruiters.

Don't let anyone throw you off by saying, "Don't worry. Tonight is just a casual evening. We're going to chat. We'll be evaluating tomorrow, during the interviews." Don't believe that for a second. Some companies will try to get you off guard — and there's never any excuse for allowing this to happen.

What Is Your Definition Of A Job Offer?
You are not assured of a job offer simply because recruiters smile, request a follow-up interview, show interest, say they will get back in touch, or tell you they like your background.

I frequently ask applicants to define an offer. Some tell me an offer is money, benefits, location, or the position, etc. The answers are usually similar, but I disagree with them. These are **components** of an offer — but still not the clear, succinct definition. An offer occurs when the **control switches hands** — when it moves from the company to you, the individual.

Prior to this point, the company is in control. They can say "yes" or "no," but **you** can't do anything. The first time you're in control is when you have the offer when you can say "yes" or "no" to the company. That's the bottom-line definition of an offer.

I've seen everything in the world happen between a recruiter's smile and the actual offer. Companies have taken an applicant through eight or nine interviews and still not offered. **Companies may say they are going to offer**, and between that time and when they could phone you, the position was filled by someone else inside the firm. Or, sometimes, the position is removed from the marketplace because of economics or internal company changes and conditions.

You should never think you have an offer until it is, in fact, in your pocket — when you're in "control."

Accepting A Career Position

This is one of the most critical moments. When you accept a position, do so with the primary person — the individual for whom you would be working or the person who made the offer. **Always accept prior to the deadline — never ever wait until the deadline.** If you do, the company doesn't know if you're accepting because time has run out or because you want the job.

Be extremely upbeat in accepting. For example, you might say, "I don't need any more time to determine I want to have my career with your company. I want you to know I'm extremely excited about getting started. What is my next step?" And, the company will go through the upcoming procedures with you.

I always tell about Janis, who now works for me. Originally, we interviewed her several times. While on a recruiting trip, I called in and learned Janis had accepted. "Is she excited?" I asked an associate. "Well, really, I don't know," I was told. "She said, 'Well, I **guess** I'll take your job.'" I was concerned about her lack of enthusiasm for the job and even suggested we call Janis back and withdraw our offer. I wanted someone more enthusiastic. Fortunately, we didn't. Janis has been with us since 1985 and is an integral part of our organization.

I wouldn't know what to do without her. But, I'll never forget her acceptance, and I've kidded her about it over the years.

Once you've accepted an offer, you should now write a letter to everyone with whom you made contact at that company. Thank them for their part — such as showing you the manufacturing facility, spending a day with you in the field, or taking time from a busy schedule to interview you and give you insight on company operations. It would be a shame if you went to work for the company, met one of the above individuals in the hall, and they didn't know you were with their firm. This is where your professional attitude in **developing relationships** should begin. It's probably one of the most critical steps in starting a company career.

Declining An Offer
When you decline an offer, don't forget your professionalism. Don't forget common courtesy. The minute you know you are not going to accept a company's offer, immediately get on the phone and let the company know. Don't send letters through the mail. That takes two or three days. Please be conscious of the fact that once an offer goes out on a position, all recruiting for that position must stop. While the company may have two or three other people in the process, they can do nothing whatsoever with them. Of course, the longer those people sit out there without being pursued, the less interest they have in that company and the higher the probability they will be hired by another company. **So, never hold an offer when you know you're not going to accept the position.**

When you decline the offer, we encourage you to be honest and candid. First of all, tell them the company you are going to join. What's the big secret? You're developing relationships in Corporate America. Let them know. Many times it is best just to say, "This was one of the most difficult decisions I've ever had to make in my life." Be honest. "But, I have made the decision to go to Company A. (Tell them who the company is.) What I'll be doing with that company is going into such and such a position. I just have to tell you the two locations were very similar, the money was very similar. I was very excited about what I saw in your company. It's just that I felt a bit more compatibility with the other firm. I don't know if I can tell you what it was. I just felt a little bit more comfortable in the other company's environment."

When you inform the company you are declining the position you have accepted, never tell them it is because of location. I'd like to go back and remind you that a company put out $3,000 to fly you in for follow-up interviews. You gave them every right to believe the location you flew out for was totally acceptable to you. So, for you to later decline because of location is to say you were dishonest and lacked professionalism. The road of life has many curves. You never know when you're going to curve back and run into that person, situation, and company again. How foolish for you to have burned a bridge when you need not have done so. Sometimes, it is simply a matter of laziness when you decline a company. What you really meant to say was, "I was sincerely open for your location. I had a preference which I pointed out in the interview. This other company has offered my location preference. It was the only factor that tipped the offer in their favor. It wasn't that your location wasn't acceptable to me. This other offer was just more acceptable." Explain your situation fully. Don't get lazy in declining an offer. Think about what you're saying. Think about your own professionalism of having accepted their money to fly out for a follow-up interview. Always be sincere and professional in any move you make in the job search.

It might even be a good idea to follow up that decline with a professional letter of thanks for all of the costs they might have incurred for your follow-up interviews and the time their managers took with you. You will certainly refer their company to other officers who are getting out of the military. **Never burn a bridge.** You never know when you may want to walk over it again.

Leave The Military Behind
When you begin your career in Corporate America, it is **very important** that you put your college and military careers behind you. Remember, what's important is not what you did yesterday, but what you are doing today.

Unfortunately, some military officers often form cliques with other officers within the companies they join. They unknowingly and unwisely create an environment of "them" versus "us." Some officers have done this to the detriment of military officers in general. Companies have told us they don't want to hire any more officers because they are becoming too "military." That is foolish when we point out that these people come from different socio-economic backgrounds, regions, cultures, and military branches. Their backgrounds are similar to young college graduates who are hired as development candidates. However, because the military officers form a clique to the exclusion of others, a perception of difference is formed.

Don't become a part of this. While you should be proud of your military service, put it behind you. Do not decorate your office with an excess of college or military memorabilia. Be more concerned about neutralizing your past and emphasizing today. It really is no more appropriate to have your grade school diploma on your office wall than it is your college diploma. These are more appropriate to decorate your den or office at home.

Working With Women

If you are a man, it is important in Corporate America that you have a positive attitude about working with women. There are officers who give us the perception that they can't work with women. Sometimes, their opinions are expressed in ways that lead us to believe they won't have good working relationships with women as peers, subordinates, or superiors. Frequently, applicants have said they spoke with one of my secretaries. When I've questioned them about whether this person said she was a secretary, they have indicated they assumed the woman was a secretary because she answered the phone.

I can relate a story which is an excellent example of this poor attitude. A recruiter called an applicant and asked him to call a woman in his office to get the details of an offer. When the applicant had received the information, he was to call the recruiter back. The applicant did as instructed and called the recruiter and said, "I called your secretary and got all the details." The recruiter then asked the applicant if the woman had identified herself as his secretary, and the applicant admitted he had just assumed she was a secretary. On the basis of this incident, the recruiter felt the applicant was biased and withdrew the job offer.

Instead of assuming the woman with whom he spoke was a secretary, the applicant could have referred to her position in a generic way. He could have said, "I spoke with your associate," or better yet — "I spoke with Ms. Anderson or Jane Anderson regarding the details." In this way, he would not have labeled her with a certain position.

I encourage you to think seriously about the roles of women and men in business. If working with women is below you or you feel women don't have the ability to compete with you, then don't apply for a position in Corporate America.

Minority Hiring/Managing Diversity

I have lived through the days when recruiting minorities was mandated by government. Major corporations were given quotas. Companies hired and promoted for the wrong reasons. We watched companies hire using double standards. There were many times when I shook my head and thought how difficult it would be to be a minority seeking employment in Corporate America.

Circumstances have changed over the years — not as fast as I feel they should have, nor as fast as many minorities think they should have. However, I can honestly say that, today, most of our great companies in Corporate America are colorblind. These companies have developed great programs to monitor minority growth. Today, there are many minorities, many I helped place, in top leadership positions in Corporate America. Is it a perfect world? It is not. I do feel, however, most of those people who are prejudiced are in the closet. They had better stay in the closet because if they stick their nose out, they're going to get it cut off. Rightfully.

I feel we're still learning how to work with minorities. I think the new theory of "managing diversity" is headed in the right direction. We are finally getting some excellent books written to help the nonminority work better with a minority and manage in a culturally diverse Corporate America. I would tell anyone coming into Corporate America with prejudice, "Please don't come." Minority groups in Corporate America are as outstanding in their productivity as anyone else. I encourage any minority to also declare yourself a minority.

I've always felt it was important to be candid, blunt, and outspoken when discussing issues with different minority groups. I think it is extremely important that you get hired for the right reason — performance — and not because you are a minority. While you may get some initial reward if you are hired as a minority, it is not the way to build a career. One should always build only on the basis of performance.

As the year 2000 approaches, demographics in the U.S. will change dramatically.
* Women will account for 47% of the workforce.
* Of all women, 61% will be employed.
* White men will account for less than 40% of the total U.S. labor force.

By the year 2010:
* The U.S. population is expected to grow by 42 million.
* Hispanics will account for 47% of the growth.
* Blacks will account for 22%.
* Asians and other people of color will account for 18%.
* Whites will account for 13%.

(Statistics from the U.S. Census Bureau.)

Managers must demonstrate the ability to manage this workforce of great diversity of backgrounds, lifestyles, values, and opinions. The "typical" employee is changing and will continue to change. U.S. corporations are challenged by the extraordinary competitive pressures in the world today. To be competitive domestically and globally will be impossible if the talents of all employees are not developed for maximum productivity. Therefore, managers will be measured by their ability to manage this diversity.

As you prepare for your interviews, be aware that you will be scrutinized for your attitudes regarding others with backgrounds different from yours. Recognize that recruiters will be looking for people who are non-judgmental, who consider others' opinions before making decisions, who value people with different backgrounds and values, and who seek to understand and accept them.

I'm proud of the large number of minorities I have brought to Corporate America. I'm proud of their tremendous success. I always feel that as you transition from the military to Corporate America, you should have some conversations with your own particular minority group. Any recruiting firm will be happy to give you references you can contact for these discussions.

CHAPTER 9

Let's Meet The Challenges Of The Future

"Roger Cameron knows what U.S. industry needs. He taught me simple techniques to make me stand out. I used his guidance in job interviews and, suddenly, I had more offers for high paying, challenging jobs than I ever expected."

— Anita Riddle
Environmental Engineer
Mobil Oil Corporation

CHAPTER 9

Let's Meet The Challenges Of The Future

Every day, companies bring to us more unique and difficult positions to fill. As a result, the military officer needs to be even more qualified. In the past, there was often limited diversity in types of positions. Today, we have a wider range of positions and career paths.

It's amazing how the demand is growing for the military officer. We've seen the ratio of openings to applicants steadily increase in every functional area such as engineering, manufacturing, marketing, sales, and data processing.

Remember, recruiters look for candidates with "BLT" — **believability, likability, and trust**. We want wholesome applicants who respect their individual qualities, but don't have to brag about them, who are tough, but not obnoxious, who are intelligent, but can work with both the intellectual and non-intellectual, and, most of all, who know how to **make it happen**, the bottom line of development candidates.

These applicants can accomplish tough, demanding objectives. They don't give excuses. Excuses are so easy to find, much easier than reaching down deep in one's self to go that extra mile.

Being Professional
Remember the definition of being **professional: a person who does what's expected of him/her — always**. This isn't an outlook that's selectively applied. It's a lifestyle. No

person can be highly successful without applying it on a full-time basis. I have to say that, in my career, I have seen a number of solid professional people. They are people who have gone up the corporate ladder very rapidly. These are people who can be counted on when they say they are going to do something. Whatever the action is that you would expect that person to take, you find they actually follow through. **If you are sincerely determined to be a success in Corporate America, do what you say you're going to do. Do what's expected of you at all times, not just when it's convenient — and even more importantly, do it when it is not convenient.**

> **Get in competitive condition
> by thorough preparation.
> Believe in yourself.
> Be positive. Think success.**

Recognizing People As Individuals
Learn to use first names. It's important. I remember interviewing in Fort Campbell, Kentucky. I'd been at a hotel near there for three days. With me was a new young recruiter who was having a hard time using first names.

The day we left, I told Betty (the waitress we usually saw in the hotel restaurant) that we were leaving. She burst into tears. Both the other recruiter and I were taken aback.

Then, she explained, "Mr. Cameron, I have to tell you how much enjoyment you've given me this week. I wear this name tag — but nobody ever calls me by my first name. Instead it's, 'Hey, waitress.' 'Hey, you.' 'Ma'am.' 'Miss.' What a pleasure to have someone recognize me as an individual." When she left, I saw that my associate was moved. And, I've never known him **not** to use first names since that experience.

Learn to do this — whether it's your gardener, a housekeeper, or the person filling your gas tank. **Recognize them as individuals**. Don't make them feel they are there simply to serve you. It will make **you** feel better, and I promise you it will make **them** feel better, too.

May I remind you that Corporate America today is a participative work environment. If you don't have the ability to work with non-intellectuals as well as intellectuals and if you don't have the ability to show that you are a people person, you frankly don't belong in Corporate America. The *FORTUNE 500* are the very best companies, and they are fanatically participative.

One of my top companies says, "If an individual doesn't have the innate ability to come to work in the morning and say, 'Good morning,' to the janitor, he or she is not the kind of person we want working for our company." You must recognize people as individuals who are worthy of your respect.

One of the nicest letters I've ever received was from an applicant I had placed with Mobil Chemical, a division of Mobil Oil. I will never forget it. He was very happy that he had chosen a great career field with a great company. With good performance, he realized that his corporate career was now essentially secure. He said the thing he really gained from our conference was the understanding of the importance of using people's first names. He went on to state how proud he was that he knew the first names of the people who put gas in his car, who did his laundry, and who served him in restaurants. Today, he never fails to look immediately at somebody's name tag and use their first name. I guess I was as proud of receiving that letter as he was of learning the importance of using first names. Please don't come to us with this excuse: "Roger, it's very difficult for me. I used 'sir' and 'ma'am' all the way through junior high, high school, and in college." We say to you, that's fine. But that was **then**, this is **now**.

If you can't convert to what it takes to be successful in Corporate America, then maybe you'd better give serious thought about taking a job in industry. We want you to be successful, but you must do it in **our** world. You must be able to **convert** in order to be successful. It's not difficult. Once you learn it, you will enjoy it. Think about how much you like hearing people use **your** first name.

Knowing How To Perform
People are the most important asset a company has. A company wants performers. Companies ask me to bring them an individual with outstanding work ethics. This is a person who gets out of bed eager to go to work — with a strong, positive mental attitude, and, most of all, the ability to **work smart**.

We've found too many officers who've had the ethic of "working smart" driven from their consciousness. They've found it impossible to plan their day or week in advance in detail. When there are sudden orders and last-minute changes, it's sometimes difficult to have a **productive** day. However, as you enter Corporate America, you must regain this skill and hone it to perfection.

It is critically important, as you make your transition to Corporate America, to demonstrate the ability to be a **peak performer**. We want smart workers, not **workaholics**. We want workers who are well-organized, know how to prioritize, and can effectively manage their time to get their work done in the minimum eight- to nine-hour work day. I honestly believe that, sometimes, the military has subconsciously issued you a set of blinders. The longer you stay in the military, the narrower and narrower your tunnel vision becomes. Is that wrong? No, not really, relative to what the military is seeking. But, it is wrong relative to what Corporate America is seeking. We want people who are constantly expanding their mind, their world, and their vision and have a lot of interests outside their job.

Don't think for a moment you're not going to work hard. During the phase when you are catching up — with those who started careers earlier — you must burn the candle at both ends and in the middle. As you reach the point where you are competitive with your age group, have gained industry knowledge, and have brought your education level to where it needs to be, then it's time to bring your work and family life into balance. Stress the **quality** of life. Don't burn yourself out on the way to the top. Work **smart**. Perform effectively. Enjoy your new career.

Controlling Your Environment
I watch people come on board as I sit in my favorite seat on Delta or American Airlines (1B or 1C). I hear them say to themselves, "What seat am I in?" Then, they moan because they are in row 35 or 39. I often think to myself, "They had an opportunity to tell the reservation clerk where they wanted to sit. Why didn't they?"

Applicants tell me they had a restless night because their room was next to the soda machine or the stairway or the ice machine. I wonder why they allow a desk clerk to put them wherever they want. Don't allow this to happen to you. Control your environment.

WE LIKE "TAKE CHARGE" PEOPLE.

Applicants give excuses why they didn't accomplish an objective. It's always somebody else's fault. "Somebody didn't let me out of work. Somebody didn't get this done." I scratch my head and say, "Why aren't you controlling your own environment?" Sure, there is no ideal system, no perfect world where we can control everything we do. You would be surprised how many things you can control if you make the effort. It will be difficult to be successful in Corporate America if you don't learn to control your environment.

I remember one of the great leaders in Corporate America. He would never let a problem come to his office except within a designated time of one half hour in the morning and one half hour in the afternoon. If the problem didn't come to him during one designated period of time, he would not handle it until the next half-hour session. He refused to allow problems or circumstances to control his environment. He was adamant about controlling his own environment. I have absolutely no doubt that's the reason he had the ability to start his career at a large company and go on to become a great leader at one of the top managed companies in the country. I learned valuable lessons from him.

Too often, I see officers who have had their lives so controlled by others that they have forgotten how to control their own destiny. So many of you tell me about the difficulty of organizing and controlling your day. I believe that. I know it's typical of so many of your jobs in the military. It is not that one environment is good and one bad. They're simply different. If you intend to come to Corporate America and be highly successful, you must **control your environment.**

> **Your performance characteristics are like staves of a barrel. Your value is worth the shortest stave. — Roger Cameron**

Let's Get Motivated

I truly believe God has given us the right to get out of bed in the morning and be happy or unhappy. It's our choice. But, there are a lot of people who must not realize they have this choice. Being in the business of recruiting and evaluating people, I observe people wherever I go — airports, hotels, athletic activities, and meetings. I have been saddened many times by people who feel the burden of the world is planted squarely on their shoulders. Whenever I have had that feeling, I have forced myself to lift my head and look at others less fortunate. I have never had to look very far — usually only within a few feet. I would then ask myself, "Do I have the right to feel sorry for myself?" Interestingly enough, 99 times out of 100, the answer was "no." I love getting out of bed in the morning. I love what I do. I love meeting people. I love the challenges that come to me every day. I like the fact that I can meet challenges head on, look them straight in the eye, and rarely fail. It's fun to be successful. It's fun to be alive. It's fun to know I can make it happen. If I visualize what I want, I can get it. I feel I am like the majority of the world's population. I have average skills. But, I have performed far above average because of one factor — desire.

I interview many outstanding men and women who have had but a fraction of the success they could have with all of their great credentials, and I think, "How sad." People come to me and tell me they should be successful because of their great abilities. I'm very quick to point out they can go to any unemployment line in America and find people with equally as much ability, maybe even more. But, because of the lack of desire to apply those abilities, they are in the unemployment line. I believe that 99.9% of them are there because they lack the desire to apply God-given abilities. I have an acquaintance who has been very successful and is quite wealthy, yet he was born with a severe handicap. We read stories, many stories, about this type of person — the individual who won't accept a physical handicap as an excuse not to be successful. Many of us complain that we don't have everything we want. We can look around and see those people who have a lot less than we have from the standpoint of intellect, appearance, or physical features. Yet, they are more successful than we are. Ever wonder why? Do you have any doubt it is simply a greater **desire** to succeed?

Many people never take responsibility for their own actions. They are the people who continually have less than great officer evaluations, and yet, none of these evaluations are their fault. They're the people who will get to the end of life, look back, and feel that life cheated them because they didn't receive everything that was due them. I disagree with all of those thoughts. I feel there is absolutely nothing you can't do if you envision your ability to do it. As I have said in this book before, you must have a make-it-happen personality. I often remember the quote, "5% of the people make it happen, 10% of the people watch things happen, and the other 85% don't care what happens." I believe this to be true. I stated earlier that, as I interview military officers around the world, I accept approximately 12%. I don't wonder why; I know why!

I often want to take young officers and say, "Are you aware you are cheating yourself? Are you aware you are letting seconds, minutes, days, weeks, and months of your life go by and not living life to the fullest? You're not reaching out to learn, grow, do, and have. Why are you doing that? Why did you get up this morning choosing to be unhappy versus happy? What was your reasoning?"

I remember being at a conference in Austin, Texas. A new corporate recruiter came to me in the middle of the day and the question was, "Roger, who pays for the applicants to come to the conference?" I said, "Of course, the applicants pay their own ways." She asked, "Who pays for their room and board?" By this time, I had no idea where she was coming from. I said, "The applicants pay for their room and board." She replied, "Well, why would a young man fly all the way from Colorado Springs to Austin to interview and show absolutely no enthusiasm or excitement. I had to turn off my air conditioner in order to hear him. He acted as if someone should give him an offer just because he showed up! As a matter of fact, I suggested to him if he thought Corporate America was simply going to hire him because of his credentials, then why was he here? Why didn't he just send a resume? After all, we could see his credentials on a resume. We would just mail him an offer or a decline through the mail." This is a true story, and one that is embarrassing to me. After all, I had recruited him to begin with — obviously, it was **my** mistake.

It is hard for me to imagine why anybody would spend $5, let alone $350 or more, to travel across the country and not accomplish the ultimate objective. This young man interviewed with 11 companies, and 11 companies declined him basically for the same reason. He just wasn't enthusiastic. He just didn't act as if he was excited to be alive. I guess he didn't believe he had a choice when he got out of bed in the morning.

As I look at applicants' interests and hobbies, I smile when I find a young officer who is reading motivational books. Few do. When this officer comes in front of me, I'm just a little bit biased. Even before I start interviewing, the applicant is a step up in the interviewing process. In 58 years of life, I couldn't begin to count all of the motivational books I have read. I can honestly tell you, I have never read one that didn't teach me something new. I also have never read one that didn't remind me of things I had failed to do in my life on a day-to-day basis.

Applicants often say, "Oh, I know all that stuff." **Knowing it** is irrelevant. The question is, **"Do you use it?** Do you really believe you can be what you want to be? Do you really believe you have the power within yourself to become a tremendous success? Do you really believe you can be a great success — not only in the military, but in Corporate America? Do you really believe you can achieve those private goals you have in your hip pocket?" I'm here to tell you that you **can** — if you really believe.

Individuals have said to me, "Well, I don't believe in motivational books. I am what I am." That's an interesting statement, isn't it? I am what I am. What these persons have just said to me and the rest of the world is that they can't improve. Whatever God created them to be, then that's the end of it. This is not true. We can improve ourselves. We can grow. Let me say again, we are adamant about finding people who are growable, people who are eager to become better. They know their success is totally within their own hands. Whatever they want to make of themselves, they can.

Rarely do I see anyone willing to spend money to improve themselves. I venture to say only two officers in a thousand actually reach in their back pocket and pay money to go to a motivational program — costing maybe $500 to $700. I immediately think back to Tim Carlin whose quote you'll find in this book. When Tim was in Germany, he involved himself in Toastmasters International — a program I recommend. This program enhanced Tim's self-confidence. He is equally at ease talking with individuals as well as speaking before large groups.

My favorite course is "The Power of Persuasion" seminar taught by Walter Hailey, Jr., of Planned Marketing Associates in Hunt, Texas. Walter is a personal friend of mine and an inspiration to me. Today, in his 60s, he has more enthusiasm than the majority of the officers I interview.

Walter teaches "Power of Persuasion" to people all over the United States and has been asked to take it to Europe. His "boot camp" is an exciting course. You cannot complete this course without knowing more about yourself. You cannot complete this course without being excited about developing your God-given talents. Anyone interested in attending his weekend course may contact our company. We'd be happy to put you in touch with him, or you'll find him written up in many periodicals and newspapers across America.

There are more than one or two courses available. There are many. Zig Ziglar does a great job of developing individuals' latent talents. So does Dale Carnegie. You don't **have** to attend a course. You can read books, rent training videos, or purchase motivational cassette tapes. However, I recommend attending the seminars in person. Interacting with others, seeing how others accomplish their goals, and meeting those from other career fields can be an additional source of knowledge and inspiration.

I love life. I enjoy working with positive, motivated people. You will never see an officer I accept who isn't excited, motivated, eager to improve, and professionally self-confident. That's exactly the quality person Corporate America is paying me to recruit.

As I reflect on the individuals I have recruited for Corporate America, all of them, with few exceptions, have been outstanding. The most dynamic and successful officers find the time to grow, learn, and broaden their knowledge base. They didn't allow some factor of life to prevent them from doing so.

If you don't have time in your life to grow, to do those types of things that make you a better person, you had better examine your life. God only gives us one chance on this earth. If I could motivate just one person who reads this book to reach down inside to find ways to improve, the book will have been a success. I have absolutely no doubt the book will make people better interviewees, but I would hope for much more than that. I would like to think the book would give you a can-do attitude. I would like to think the book would allow you to choose the best of the two options you have every morning and live it. Remember, when life is over and you look back, no one will have cheated you if you have not accomplished what you had hoped to accomplish. You will have cheated yourself. Don't let that happen. Every day that goes by is a day you will never be able to live over again.

Tomorrow morning, when you wake up and have the choice to make it a good day or a bad day, make the right decision. I know an individual who every morning when she leaves her bedroom, crosses an imaginary line on the floor outside her bedroom door. As she crosses that line, she is consciously aware it is her choice to make her day whatever she wants it to be. I have rarely seen her not accomplish her objective.

Every day is a positive day. She is motivated. She accomplishes difficult objectives. At the end of the day, she feels good about reaching the goals she has established for herself. Put that imaginary line outside of your bedroom door. Be conscious of your choices as you step across it every day.

In conclusion, I strongly recommend you take firm control. Be a catalyst and motivate yourself to accomplish the objectives you want for yourself and your family. Read motivational books. Listen to motivational tapes. Consider spending some money early in your career on seminars to learn from some of the very best America has to offer. Most of all, when you wake up in the morning, be sure you make the right decision.

Marching Orders
During the course of this book, I have suggested ways to handle certain questions and situations. **Under no circumstances am I suggesting that you use my words**. Every thought and every idea should be digested and put into your **own** words, your own manner of delivery. No recruiter wants a person to use someone else's words. There may be certain cases where words are used from a phrase, but we encourage applicants to be themselves. You are a unique individual, and you must interview as that unique individual.

I want you to remember that you're an outstanding individual in your own right. This book has been designed to improve your interviewing ability — not to necessarily change you as an individual. I encourage you to give serious thought to what you want to do with your life. If that means coming to Corporate America or having a career in a different field, this book will help you (regardless of the field).

I feel you have several selves — you at your best, you at your average, and you at your worst. Interview at your best. To be your best at anything you do, you must be thoroughly prepared. Be committed to what you're doing; focus and concentrate on your objective.

I encourage you to start early to prepare for any difficult objective. Don't wait until the last minute. Prepare as early as you can in your career for any potential changes you might make. Be conscious, as you go through your military career, of what you do specifically, individually, and uniquely, to motivate subordinates. While the military gives you leadership guidance, they don't restrict you from personalizing methods of motivation. Be conscious of the individual people problems you have solved along the way. Be performance-oriented. Be conscious of non-people problems you've solved and know how you've solved them. Be aware of the skills you use — organizational ability, prioritizing, effective time management, etc. — and the procedure you go through each time you solve any problem.

Use a tape recorder to verbalize answers before you get in front of the colonel, the general, or anyone else. Never be embarrassed by the fact that you must practice to be concise and articulate. Preparation for anything you do in life only makes you a better person. I've never heard of anyone who gained success in becoming a better officer, a better marksman, a better skier, or a better speaker without practice. I've never known preparation to be embarrassing. All I have ever heard in my 58 years of living is, "Boy, that person really worked hard to be successful." That's right. That's exactly what it takes.

Come to Corporate America with a high degree of enthusiasm. Have self-confidence and poise in knowing yourself. I encourage you to become consciously aware of who you are. Have accurate self-insight. Be able to communicate in a forceful manner so we will not only hear what you say, but we will believe it as well.

Know what you have done in the military and what has made you successful. The better you know yourself, the better you know how you have accomplished difficult objectives and the better you can apply that formula to any career objective — in Corporate America, civil service, or your own business.

I hope you've enjoyed this book. I hope you feel better prepared now that you have read it. However, no one book makes a well-read applicant. I encourage you to read other outstanding books on Corporate America. You can go to any bookstore and find a host of books to read. If you have true enthusiasm for a career in Corporate America, it is very easy to learn about it. You can go into any Holiday Inn, Sheraton, or Marriott and meet business people at the lunch table. Introduce yourself. Tell them who you are. I've never known anyone in Corporate America who wouldn't take the time to explain what industry is all about. They'll be happy to talk to you and give you some insight. Take advantage of every opportunity. Best of luck to you!

To All Military Officers:

Cameron-Brooks is available to discuss and evaluate your marketability. We will tell you the dollar value of your credentials and the probable career field for which you are qualified. You can be assured of a candid evaluation and extremely knowledgeable, constructive advice.

I strongly encourage you to contact us early in your career. We will then have the opportunity to suggest certain skill enhancements, additional formal education, specific military assignments, and the best time for you to transition into Corporate America with your particular skills.

Your early acceptance will enable you to further develop your skills through our development and preparation program which is regarded as the very best transitional training available. The more time you spend with us, the more marketable you become, and the smoother your transition will be. We continually receive outstanding comments about our preparation program — not only in terms of interviewing skill development, but the long-term positive effect it has on an officer's career.

Most importantly, our services come to you at no charge.

As the leader in military recruitment, we know our business. We know what it takes, having successfully recruited officers with backgrounds from engineering to liberal arts. Our diverse alumni base includes positions from design engineering, information systems, manufacturing and operations, to sales and marketing. We have recruited officers for these positions in every industry in Corporate America. Our reputation is established on both sides of our business — the military officer and the companies we represent.

Above all, we are acknowledged for the professional, caring involvement our entire Cameron-Brooks Team devotes to each of our military officers. We sincerely care about you and your careers and welcome the opportunity to form a partnership dedicated to your success. In fact, we say that the best measurement of our success is your success.

Call or write us today. Together, we can "make it happen!"

Roger Cameron

Appendix A

DEFINITIONS OF CRITICAL CHARACTERISTICS

Assertiveness: your ability to take charge and present opinions forcefully and persuasively. Many individuals say the right thing, but not in a believable manner.

Conflict/Resolution: your ability to settle differences of opinion while maintaining good relationships and attaining goals with peers, superiors, and subordinates alike.

Decision-Making: your thought process (conceptual and analytical) used in problem solving and exercising good judgment. Your ability to make decisions is often brought out in interviews through the use of "why" questions.

Decisiveness: your willingness to commit yourself and when asked, make definite choices; your ability to demonstrate where you stand on issues; not tentative.

Energy/Enthusiasm: your animation, demonstrated by your walk, handshake, and verbal vitality.

Goal Setting/Accomplishments: your ability to establish and achieve meaningful, attainable objectives, overcoming adversity if necessary.

Initiative: your active efforts to influence events rather than passively accepting them; self-starting, not needing constant prompting from superiors.

Innovativeness/Creativeness: your ability to be visionary and to keep your eye on the big picture versus having tunnel vision. The desire and ability to move into unchartered waters. Without these two traits, you are a follower instead of a leader.

Intelligence: your conceptual ability, breadth of knowledge, verbal expression, depth of response, analytical thought process.

Interpersonal Skill: your ability to develop a spontaneous, conversational relationship.

Maturity: your capacity to exercise emotional control and self-discipline, and your ability to behave realistically. Youth is unfairly and frequently associated with immaturity. You will always have the burden of proof in all interviews.

Openness: your ability to discuss shortcomings as well as strengths, to not be preoccupied with saying the right thing, and to be consistently responsive regardless of content. Recruiters don't want to wonder if there is a hidden meaning to your words. We hire people who "lay the cards on the table" tactfully and professionally.

Oral Communication Skills: your effectiveness of expression; your ability to deliver in a fluid, articulate, succinct, and persuasive manner.

Planning/Organization: your effectiveness in arranging your own activities and those of a group. Your ability to establish an effective, efficient cause of action.

Poise/Self-Confidence: your ease in communicating positively during the interview. Recruiters want to see that you are comfortable under pressure.

Self-Insight: your ability to accurately and introspectively perceive, understand, and communicate your strengths and weaknesses.

Sensitivity: your sincerity, friendliness, tactfulness, and responsiveness; your ability to **listen** as well as speak. Be sensitive to recruiters' signals, such as diverting their eyes, shuffling papers, or constantly looking at their watches. They will always give you signals.

Team Player: your ability to function in a group environment; your demonstrated attitude of ensuring success to those around you equal to your own.

Tough-mindedness: your ability to make strong, firm, emotionally difficult business and people decisions.

Appendix B

RECOMMENDED READING LIST

Corporate America wants broad-minded, well-read managers. You must develop depth and breadth, and reading is a critical step toward achieving greater success.

The books and periodicals listed here are very current in business, and I recommend them to you. However, they are **under no circumstances** the only ones you should read. Following each title are comments which explain why I feel the book or periodical is important.

1. **Magazines and Newspapers**

    A. *FORTUNE.* I recommend *FORTUNE* over *The Wall Street Journal, Business Week, Forbes*, and others because it focuses on the trenches of industry, where you'll start, as opposed to corporate finance and merger and acquisition news. The others are excellent, but just not as immediately applicable.

    B. *USA Today.* Good for a broad-brush national news review.

    C. *A Regional Newspaper.* To complement *USA Today*, it helps to understand regional and local news. Shy away from small-town locals and find a metropolitan-based daily (Atlanta, Dallas, Washington, D.C.). Often, these major dailies have a "Week in Review" section on Sunday that provides a great synopsis.

2. **General Business Books**

    A. *In Search of Excellence* (Peters and Waterman). A must read for all. It prescribes eight principles that, while apparently common sense, are in use in only the "best" companies. This book uses personal examples and is very easy to read — even fun. This book has transcended the best-seller list to become a classic.

B. *A Passion for Excellence* (Peters and Austin). This book and *Search* are virtually always mentioned as a two-volume set, but fewer have read *Passion*, and it is, in fact, more useful. It will give you specific ways to implement ideas voiced in *Search*. Pay attention to "Things To Do Now."

C. *Thriving On Chaos* (Peters). This Tom Peters book addresses ways to adapt to the changing world business climate and is an easy read.

D. *The Renewal Factor* (Waterman). *Renewal* is written to the same issues as *Thriving,* but with (again) eight themes divided into sections. This may become a classic.

E. *GMP: The Greatest Management Principle in the World* (LeBoeuf). Once you read it, you'll realize how uncommon it is to see common sense in practice. This book is easy to read, short, and fun.

F. *Dress for Success* and *The Woman's Dress for Success* (Molloy). You will not make it if you don't dress the part, and I think you may be surprised at how many misconceptions you have. Refer to it as you build your wardrobe. Always remember to err (if you must) on the conservative side.

G. *Reinventing the Corporation* (Naisbitt and Aburdene). This book is very interesting and forward-thinking, and it will help you switch gears and start thinking like your future peers in industry. It also sheds excellent light on the expanding role of women in industry and corporate involvement in quality of life issues.

H. *World Class Manufacturing* (Schonberger). A must read for all manufacturing and operations candidates. This book, and the principles it espouses, is on the lips of virtually all of the forward-thinking corporations. You must understand Total Quality and Just In Time (JIT) concepts.

I. *Japanese Manufacturing Techniques* (Schonberger). In a clear, handbook format are nine "lessons" for American manufacturers, introducing scores of techniques aimed at simplifying the overly-complex purchasing, inventory, assembly-line, and quality-control processes of U.S. firms.

J. *Self-Directed Work Teams* (Orsburn, Moran, Musselwhite, Zenger). In today's dynamic marketplace, only the agile and lean survive. *Self-Directed Work Teams* shows you how to boost productivity, improve the quality of your product or service, and thrive on competition. Don't even think about interviewing in Manufacturing without understanding these principles.

K. *Total Quality* (The Ernst & Young Quality Improvement Consulting Group). The primary purpose of the book is to offer a succinct yet comprehensive guide for management who must lead what amounts to a cultural transformation. Implementing cultural changes requires a very different leader from the traditional U.S. leadership model. The book describes not only what the manager must know, but also what he or she must do to help accomplish this radical change.

L. *Quality Without Tears* (Crosby). All applicants, especially those considering manufacturing, must appreciate Corporate America's focus on quality. The real key to profitability is not inspection, but prevention.

M. *Strategic Selling* (Miller and Herman). Considered the best professional approach to selling in many years, it will virtually give you a master's in selling overnight. Highly recommended by many *FORTUNE 100* companies, this is mandatory reading for applicants considering sales & marketing.

N. *Spin Selling* (Rackham). $1 million research into effective sales performance is the best-documented account of sales success ever collected. No other book written does as good a job of analyzing different types of sales. I strongly recommend for those having some sales experience.

O. *The Other Guy Blinked* (Enrico). This book is a wonderful business story of how Pepsi beat Coca Cola in the cola wars that started a few years ago. It is fun and easy to read. The book is very enlightening to those aspiring to a career in marketing.

P. *The Black Manager* (Dickens and Dickens). An outstanding book for Blacks going into Corporate America, for Blacks being managed by Whites, and Whites being managed by Blacks. Floyd Dickens speaks from a very successful career with Procter & Gamble. We strongly recommend its valuable insight.

And, finally, four classics that stand by themselves, and that everyone should read, keep, and refer to:

Q. *How to Win Friends and Influence People* (Carnegie). Everybody has heard of this one. While many have read it, not all have put it into action. It is outstanding and gives you specific suggestions for improvement. Read annually.

R. *The Power of Positive Thinking* (Peale). Any high achiever will tell you that you must think positively **first** to get positive results. Visualize success and it will happen.

S. *Top Performance* (Ziglar). Actually, anything by Ziglar is great reading as a motivational book, but this one gives you plenty of tools and tips to beat the competition.

T. *The 7 Habits of Highly Effective People* (Covey). Discover how to free yourself from the weaknesses of others while taking responsibility for your own life. A must read.

RECOMMENDED SEMINARS AND TAPES

Seminars:

The following are names and addresses of presenters as well as a listing of some of the seminars they offer:

- Topics:
  The Power of Persuasion
  Career
  Time Management
  Presenters: Walter Hailey and Steve Anderson

  Planned Marketing Associates
  P. O. Box 345
  Hunt, Texas 78024
  1-800-749-7621

- Topics:
  The Psychology of Leadership
  Success Secrets of High Achievers
  Presenter: Brian Tracy

  Brian Tracy Learning Systems
  462 Stevens Avenue, Suite 202
  Solana Beach, California 92075-2065

- Topics:
  The Psychology of Winning
  The Winner's Edge
  Winning for Life
  Being the Best
  The New Dynamics of Winning: Gaining the Mindset of a Champion
  Presenter: Denis Waitley

  Denis Waitley, Inc.
  P. O. Box 197
  Rancho Santa Fe, California 92067
  1-619-756-4201, 1-619-756-5969
  FAX 1-619-756-9717

- Topics:
  See You at the Top
  How to Stay Motivated
  Presenter: Zig Ziglar

  Zig Ziglar Corporation
  3330 Earhart Drive, #204
  Carrollton, Texas 75006-5026
  1-214-233-9191
  1-800-527-0306

- Topic: *Increasing Human Effectiveness II*
  Presenter: Bob Moawad

  Edge Learning Institute
  2217 N. 30th Street
  Tacoma, Washington 98403
  1-206-272-3103
  Outside Washington: 1-800-858-1484

The following videos and audiotapes emphasize self-improvement and are available through the Nightingale-Conant Corporation, 7300 North Lehigh Avenue, Chicago, Illinois 60648-9951.

Videotapes:

- *The Magic Word: Attitude* by Earl Nightingale
  Videocassette (43 min.) with two audiocassettes and two guides. Teaches you how to develop and maintain your game plan for success — a good attitude.

- *GOALS: Setting and Achieving Them on Schedule* by Zig Ziglar
  Videocassette (70 min.) helps you receive and set your goals and write your "business plan for life."

- *The Master Key to Success* by Napoleon Hill
  Two videocassettes and four audiocassettes with workbook. Provides classic achievement principles that show success is no accident.

Audiotapes:

- *The Psychology of Achievement* by Brian Tracy
  Six tapes plus workbook. Teaches seven basic laws of achievement. Helps you identify your "area of excellence."

- *The Power of Positive Thinking* by Norman Vincent Peale
  Six audiocassettes with Listener's Guide. An all-time classic to help you increase your confidence in what you can accomplish.

- *Working Smarter* by Michael LeBoeuf
  Six audiocassettes. More than a time management system. Provides specific instructions, simple systems, and valuable psychological tips.

- *The Psychology of Winning* by Denis Waitley
  Six audiocassettes with Progress Guide. Provides ten steps to winning that you can immediately use in every area of your life.

- *The Courage to Live Your Dreams* by Les Brown
  Six audiocassettes. Focuses on how to build good self-esteem by developing a strong vision of yourself and by using positive self-talk.

- *Unlimited Power* by Anthony Robbins
  Six audiocassettes. Contains techniques for breaking self-destructive habits, erasing negative thought patterns and achieving peak performance.

- *Think and Grow Rich* by Napoleon Hill
  Eight audiocassettes, hard-cover book, study guide and owner's manual. Presents practical, money-making principles used by very successful people.

Appendix C

BEHAVIORAL TRAITS

Use this list to help you determine your behavioral traits.

ABSOLUTE	ENERGETIC	POSITIVE
ASSERTIVE	EXCEPTIONAL	PRODUCTIVE
ASTUTE	EXPLICIT	PROFICIENT
"BLT"	FARSIGHTED	PROFOUND
BRIGHT	FOCUSED	PRUDENT
CALCULATING	FORCEFUL	QUICK
CATEGORICAL	FRIENDLY	RATIONAL
CERTAIN	GENIAL	REASONABLE
CLEAR	GENUINE	RELENTLESS
CLEAR-HEADED	GRITTY	RESOURCEFUL
COGNIZANT	HARD WORKER	RESPONSIVE
COMMON SENSE	HONEST	SENSIBLE
COMPETENT	IMAGINATIVE	SENSITIVE
COMPETITIVE	INDOMITABLE	SERIOUS
COMPOSED	INFLUENTIAL	SHARP
CONFIDENT	INGENIOUS	SHREWD
CONSCIENTIOUS	INNOVATIVE	SINCERE
CONSISTENT	INSISTENT	SKILLFUL
CONVERSATIONAL	INTELLIGENT	SMART
CONVINCING	INTENSE	SOLID
CREATIVE	INVENTIVE	STRONG-MINDED
CURIOUS	KEEN	STRONG-WILLED
DECIDED	LEADER	SURE
DECISIVE	LIVELY	TACTFUL
DETERMINED	MAGNETIC	TEAM PLAYER
DEXTEROUS	"MAKE-IT-HAPPEN"	TENACIOUS
DISCERNING	NOTABLE	THOUGHTFUL
DOGMATIC	OPEN	TOUGH-MINDED
DYNAMIC	PERCEPTIVE	UNFLINCHING
EARNEST	PERSUASIVE	VIGOROUS
EFFICIENT	PLUCKY	VITAL
EMPHATIC	POISED	WISE

Appendix D

Appendix D

INTERVIEW SELF-EVALUATION

I strongly recommend that you evaluate your presentation before and after each interview to help immediately identify deficiencies. Companies want to hire Top Performers. You demonstrate your ability to become a Top Performer when you interview at a Perfect 10 level.

- **Before** each interview, review these key factors and focus on perfect performance.
- **After** each interview, "Rate Your Performance!" Analyze how you can improve the next time! Be critical.

When you can confidently rank at an overall Perfect Top 10 Performance Level, you are on the road to success . . . .

You can only rank yourself a 10 when each factor in the box is a 10!

Circle 5-10 (Perfect = 10)

IMPRESSION		**INTERPERSONAL SKILLS**	
• Smile	• Appearance	• Establish rapport	• Relate/Respond
• Handshake	• Walk	• Curiosity	• Connect
• Energy	• Posture/Poise	• Listen Actively	• Sincere
• Eye Contact	• FOCUS	• Approachable	• FOCUS
...5 6 7 8 9 10		...5 6 7 8 9 10	

COMMUNICATION		**CONFIDENCE**	
• Persuasive	• Body Language	• Convincing	• Knowledgeable
• Articulate	• Good Answers	• Positive	• Self-Assured
• Listen	• Good Questions	• Competitive	• Use names
• Relate Assets	• FOCUS	• Eye Contact	• FOCUS
...5 6 7 8 9 10		...5 6 7 8 9 10	

CLOSE	
• Company Specific	• Believable
• FOCUS	
...5 6 7 8 9 10	

How would you rank yourself overall? ...5 6 7 8 9 10	**MAKE IT A PERFECT 10!**	How would the recruiter rank you? ...5 6 7 8 9 10

Appendix E

John Q. Citizen
Street Address
City, State Nine Digit Zip Code
(Area Code) Home Phone Number

AVAILABLE: January 1, 1994
Age: 28; 5'10"; 180 lbs.
Married

EDUCATION
BS Electrical Engineering 1985
University of Southern California
Los Angeles, California

MBA Finance 1993
Loyola College in Maryland
Baltimore, Maryland

ACTIVITIES
High School: Valedictorian; County Student of the Month; Rotary Club Outstanding Senior; Student of the Year; National Honor Society; Class President; Student Government Representative (Treasurer); Presidential Classroom for Young Americans; Boys State; Key Club (Treasurer, Lieutenant Governor 17th District); Alliance Area Youth Center President; Varsity Basketball; Varsity Football; Worked part-time 6 hours per week during school and full-time 60 hours per week during summers.
College: Graduated with Distinction; Immediate Graduate Education Program; Tau Beta Pi Engineering Honor Society; American Society of Naval Engineers; American Nuclear Society (Student Paper Finalist).
Note: 50% of undergraduate education financed by scholarship, 25% by loans, and 25% by part-time work. 100% of graduate degree financed by full-time work.

EXPERIENCE: 6/85-Present – Captain, Field Artillery, United States Army

7/89-Present Damage Control Assistant/Quality Assurance Officer: Responsible for maintenance and repair of all auxiliary mechanical and electrical systems on nuclear submarine, including: diesel engine, hydraulic power plants, compressed air, atmospheric control, refrigeration, electronic cooling, plumbing, interior communications, and damage control equipment. Supervise 13 mechanics and 5 electricians.
* Noted as "having the best ship's fire drill ever seen" during Operational Reactor Safeguards Examination.
* Qualified 12 quality assurance inspectors and 11 controlled material petty officers within 6 months which was noted by Nuclear Propulsion Examining Board as "Superior" to other submarines.
* Established Quality Assurance Audit and Surveillance Program which was evaluated by Nuclear Propulsion Plant Examining Board as "Outstanding."

12/87-6/89 Company Commander: Responsible for training and welfare of 85 communication-electronic intelligence technicians and over 20 families, with mission of providing voice collection and electronic jamming support. Responsible for maintenance of 12 high technology computerized intelligence collection systems and 44 wheeled vehicles.
* Won Community Commander's Sports Cup over 15 other companies.
* Recognized as "Best" ground based intelligence unit in Europe.
* Maintained 95% maintenance rate, 5% above Army standard.
* Only company of 4 to receive "Fully Trained" rating during Command Inspection.
* Selected for command while junior Captain in brigade.

9/86-11/87 Anti-Satellite (ASAT) Test Data Analysis Manager: Directed data collection, pre-flight and post-flight data processing, and analysis for all ASAT flight tests. Managed 30-member data analysis team responsible for determining real-time system health status. Responsible for 100+ post-flight data products.
* Led real-time and post-test data analysis for successful first intercept of an orbiting satellite.
* Reduced post-flight analysis time line by 15% by creating tracking system that identified time-critical data products and negotiated improved delivery schedules.
* Created navigation analysis computer program which eliminated costly additional product.

6/85-8/86 Company Executive Officer: Responsible for supervising maintenance program and general operation of Bradley equipped, infantry Rifle Company consisting of 109 soldiers, 14 armored vehicles, and 4 wheeled vehicles. Responsible for monitoring supply functions, logistical support, and combat readiness, and for assisting commander in tactical operations.
* Raised company maintenance operational readiness rate from 50% to 92% after 4 months in position, 3% over objective.
* Increased average gunnery scores by 10%.
* Received "Commendable" rating of 93% on Division Readiness Test.
* Achieved highest gunnery score in battalion with 960 point average, increase of 6%.
* Attended 4 months of Infantry Officer Training, Commandant's List.

John Q. Citizen
Street Address
City, State Nine Digit Zip Code
(Area Code) Home Phone Number

AVAILABLE: January 1, 1994
Age: 28; 5'10"; 180 lbs.
Married

OBJECTIVE: Manufacturing Manager

EDUCATION
BS Electrical Engineering 1985
University of Southern California
Los Angeles, California

MBA Finance 1993
Loyola College in Maryland
Baltimore, Maryland

EXPERIENCE: 6/85-Present – Captain, Field Artillery, United States Army

7/89-Present Damage Control Assistant/Quality Assurance Officer: Responsible for maintenance and repair of all auxiliary mechanical and electrical systems on nuclear submarine, including diesel engine, hydraulic power plants, compressed air, atmospheric control, refrigeration, electronic cooling, plumbing, interior communications, and damage control equipment. Supervise 13 mechanics and 5 electricians.
* Noted as "having the best ship's fire drill ever seen" during Operational Reactor Safeguards Examination.
* Qualified 12 quality assurance inspectors and 11 controlled material petty officers within 6 months which was noted by Nuclear Propulsion Examining Board as "Superior" to other submarines.
* Established Quality Assurance Audit and Surveillance Program which was evaluated by Nuclear Propulsion Plant Examining Board as "Outstanding."

12/87-6/89 Company Commander: Responsible for training and welfare of 85 communication-electronic intelligence technicians and over 20 families, with mission of providing voice collection and electronic jamming support. Responsible for maintenance of 12 high technology computerized intelligence collection systems and 44 wheeled vehicles.
* Won Community Commander's Sports Cup over 15 other companies.
* Recognized as "Best" ground based intelligence unit in Europe.
* Maintained 95% maintenance rate, 5% above Army standard.
* Only company of 4 to receive "Fully Trained" rating during Command Inspection.
* Selected for command while junior Captain in brigade.

9/86-11/87 Anti-Satellite (ASAT) Test Data Analysis Manager: Directed data collection, pre-flight and post-flight data processing, and analysis for all ASAT flight tests. Managed 30-member data analysis team responsible for determining real-time system health status. Responsible for 100+ post-flight data products.
* Led real-time and post-test analysis for successful first intercept of an orbiting satellite.
* Reduced post-flight analysis time line by 15% by creating tracking system that identified time-critical data products and negotiated improved delivery schedules.
* Created navigation analysis computer program which eliminated costly additional product.

6/85-8/86 Company Executive Officer: Responsible for supervising maintenance program and general operation of Bradley equipped, infantry Rifle Company consisting of 109 soldiers, 14 armored vehicles, and 4 wheeled vehicles. Responsible for monitoring supply functions, logistical support, and combat readiness, and for assisting commander in tactical operations.
* Raised company maintenance operational readiness rate from 50% to 92% after 4 months in position, 3% over objective.
* Increased average gunnery scores by 10%.
* Received "Commendable" rating of 93% on Division Readiness Test.
* Achieved highest gunnery score in battalion with 960 point average, increase of 6%.
* Attended 4 months of Infantry Officer Training, Commandant's List.

INDEX

For further information about our career services, please complete the reverse side of the response card found below, or contact us directly at:

Cameron-Brooks, Inc.
Training & Consulting Division
Pfiester Road
P.O. Box 839
Fredericksburg, TX   78624-0839

1-800-444-9832

- -

CAMERON-BROOKS, INC.

BUSINESS REPLY MAIL
FIRST-CLASS MAIL PERMIT NO. 42 FREDERICKSBURG TX

POSTAGE WILL BE PAID BY ADDRESSEE

CAMERON-BROOKS, INC.
PFIESTER ROAD
P.O. BOX 839
FREDERICKSBURG, TX   78624-9972

At Cameron-Brooks, we are dedicated to your career success. If you are interested in more information about our books or professional recruiting services, please indicate those items in which you are interested by checking the corresponding box number on the post card below, detach the card, and forward it to our office. You may also call toll-free, 1-800-444-9832, if you would like to speak to one of our representatives.

I am interested in knowing more about:
1.　　　*Your Career Fast Track Starts In College*
2.　　　*PCS To Corporate America*
3.　　　Cameron-Brooks' Professional Recruiting Services

I am interested in sharing your books and services with a friend. Please forward the indicated information to the address I have shown below.
4.　　　*Your Career Fast Track Starts In College*
5.　　　*PCS To Corporate America*
6.　　　Cameron-Brooks' Professional Recruiting Services

Thank you for your interest!
We sincerely hope that this book has helped you
attain your career goals.

— — — — — — — — — — Cut along this line — — — — — — — — — —

CAMERON-BROOKS, INC.
TRAINING AND CONSULTING DIVISION

No postage required
if mailed in the U.S.
or from
APO/FPO address.

1. ☐　　2. ☐　　3. ☐　　4. ☐　　5. ☐　　6. ☐
Check the box/es, (☑) which correspond/s to the information listed above.

<u>Your contact information:</u>

Name: ——————————————
Address:——————————————
　　　　　　　　　　Zip: —————

Home Phone: —————————————

Work Phone: —————————————

<u>Your friend's information:</u>

Name: ——————————————
Address: ——————————————
　　　　　　　　　　Zip: —————

Home Phone: —————————————

Work Phone: —————————————

Cameron-Brooks, Inc.　☆　Training & Consulting Division
Pfiester Road, P.O. Box 839　☆　Fredericksburg, Texas　78624-0839